# SPIRITUAL
# LESSONS

# SPIRITUAL LESSONS

*by*

J. OSWALD SANDERS

An Overseas Missionary Fellowship Book
(formerly China Inland Mission)

**MOODY PRESS**
CHICAGO

© 1944 by J. Oswald Sanders

MOODY PRESS REVISED EDITION, 1971


Original Title:
SPIRITUAL PROBLEMS


ISBN: 0-8024-0106-6

# CONTENTS

# PREFACE TO THE REVISED EDITION

This small volume contains suggested solutions to fifteen problems of the inner life of the Christian who has set out on the highway of holiness. With the growing complexity of life, problems do not tend to decrease. Indeed, the young people of today are subjected to pressures and temptations far more intense than was the case a generation ago. They are therefore in more urgent need of an answer to their recurring problems. It is the author's conviction that every perplexity has its satisfying answer in the spiritual laws and principles enunciated in the Scriptures. The method adopted is therefore mainly expository. Testimonies to blessing received through previous editions have encouraged the issue of this revised edition.

J. OSWALD SANDERS

Go to God Himself, and ask for the calling of God; for as certainly as He has a plan or calling for you, He will somehow guide you into it. . . . By this hidden union with God, or intercourse with Him, we get a wisdom or insight deeper than we know ourselves; a sympathy, a oneness with the Divine will and love. We go into the very plan of God for us, and are led along in it by Him, consenting, co-operating, answering to Him, and working out with nicest exactness that good end for which His unseen counsel girded us and sent us into the world. In this manner we can never be greatly at a loss to find our way into God's counsel and plan. The duties of the present moment we shall meet as they rise, and these will open a gate into the next, and we shall thus pass on trustfully and securely, almost never in doubt as to what God calls us to do. . . .

All men living without God are adventurers out upon God's world, in neglect of Him, to choose their own course. Hence the sorrowful sad-looking host they make. Oh, that I could shew them whence their dryness, their unutterable sorrows come. Oh, that I could silence for one hour the noisy tumult of their works and get them to look in upon that better, higher life of fruitfulness and blessing to which their God has appointed them.

HORACE BUSHNELL

# 1

# THE LESSON OF GUIDANCE

> I will instruct thee and teach thee in the way which
> thou shalt go: I will guide thee with mine eye (Ps
> 32:8).

Is it possible to enjoy divine direction in life, in its
broad highways and in its byways? Has God a plan for
the life of each Christian? Can we know beyond doubt
that we are moving in the direction of the will of God?

These are questions of more than academic interest.
To the one who desires to know God's highest for him,
they are of vital importance. If there is no ideal and individual plan for each life, then each must devise his
own and work toward it. If there is such an ideal plan,
then he must renounce his own planning and diligently
set himself to discover and execute God's plan.

Nothing is more tragic than a misdirected life, a life
which has failed of its early promise and become a mis-
fit. A wrong step in matrimony, or a choice made at the
cross roads of life has engulfed many a Christian in suffering and tragedy. But such catastrophes need not be
repeated for there is guidance and direction for all.

## Guidance Is Promised

The plain fact is that not everyone who professes to
seek guidance is honestly desirous of being guided into
God's will. An architect complains that many of his

clients ask him to design a home for them, only to let him speedily discover that they have already designed it for themselves. What they really desire is that he sanction *their* plan. They want the satisfaction of seeing him draw on paper what they have already decided upon. In very much the same fashion we sometimes go to the great Architect of our lives. We ask Him for wisdom and guidance, but we have already decided how we will shape our course. It is not His way we are seeking, but His approval of *our* way.

But to those who sincerely desire His direction, the Scriptures afford satisfying testimony to the fact that God is arranging and controlling with meticulous care the minutest detail of the life of the one who submits to His guidance. Scripture is replete with such assurances.

> The LORD shall guide thee continually (Is 58:11).
> The steps of a good man are ordered by the LORD (Ps 37:23).
> In all thy ways acknowledge him, and he shall direct thy paths (Pr 3:6).
> We are his workmanship, created . . . unto good works, which God hath before ordained that we should walk in them (Eph 2:10).

If these scriptures mean what they appear to say, we must accept it as axiomatic that from this moment God has an ideal plan for the remainder of our lives in which He seeks our cooperation. The past with its failures is irretrievable, its opportunities have fled beyond recall. But failure need never be final. Our Guide gives an assurance full of encouragement: "I will restore unto you the years that the locust hath eaten" (Joel 2:25). To the penitent heart He gives renewed opportunity. From this moment, if we invite Him, He will take the helm, and with unerring skill steer the bark of our lives through hidden rocks and treacherous shoals to the desired haven.

While it is perfectly true that God has a perfect plan, He does not usually disclose to us more than the next step in it. The fact of His guidance does not dispense with the necessity for the exercise of faith. It must surely have been mystifying to Joseph when the divine plan led him from his father's home to the bear pit, and thence to the far country and finally to an Egyptian dungeon. Yet, viewing it from its close, he could trace his God's loving direction in every step along the way which led ultimately to the throne. He exclaimed exultantly to his apprehensive brothers, "So it was not you that sent me hither, but God" (Gen 45:8). To all outward appearances his path led down, down, down to shameful obscurity. But effluxion of time demonstrated that instead it led up, up, up to honor and power and wealth. "He that followeth me shall not walk in darkness" is the divine promise (Jn 8:12). But it is also true that he who will not have God as guide must grope his way as best he can.

Thomas Carlyle once said, "Of all paths a man could strike into, there is, at any given moment, a best path for every man—a thing which here and now it were of all things wisest for him to do; which, could he be led or driven to do, he were then doing like a man as we phrase it. His success in such a case were complete, his felicity a maximum." The man who discovers and follows God's plan for his life cannot be other than successful and joyous in the true sense of those terms.

## GUIDANCE IS IMPERATIVE

"It is not in man that walketh to direct his steps" (Jer 10:23).

The consensus of human experience confirms this categorical affirmation. Innumerable wrecked lives bear eloquent though mute witness to man's inability to shape his own destiny, to guide his own bark. Daily guidance is an indispensable necessity as well as a wonderful privilege for us.

Life is one long succession of choices between the right and the wrong, the better and the best. Two paths open before us. Each looks equally alluring at the fork. We must walk one of them. But which? More than human wisdom and insight is needed, for the path ahead is so obscure, our vision so defective, and our wisdom so limited. The disposition of events is not in our hands but in God's. He alone can tell what the next hour holds, and therefore He alone is competent to direct our steps.

Again, we are not alone on the road. The Christian is surrounded with hostile and supernatural forces of which he is all too unconscious and ignorant: "the despotisms, the powers, the world rulers of this present darkness, the spirit forces of wickedness in the heavenly sphere" (Eph 6:12 par). But while we may be ignorant of the devices of our adversary, they all lie exposed to our heavenly Guide who will lead us safely through.

Both physical and spiritual consequences in maladjusted and misdirected lives are so serious as to make correct orientation to the will of God a matter of all-consuming importance. In a speech before the British Association, it was stated that of five hundred consecutive cases of nervous and mental illness, overwork was an important causal factor in only 2 percent. In the vast majority of cases the causes were more personal and had to do much less with external stress and strain than with personal unhappiness and conflict within the mind. Finding the plan of God and conforming to it result in inner harmony. Missing it inevitably produces inner discord.

### GUIDANCE IS INDIVIDUAL

In guidance God does not treat us as robots but as intelligent and responsible beings. He does not deal with men in the mass but has individual and personal transactions with each. Since each person is distinctive and unique in the world, God has as many methods and plans as He has men. In His dealings no detail of heredity or environment, of temperament or talent is left out of account. Infinite knowledge plans with infinite sympathy and understanding.

Among young people especially there is the tendency to indulge vain regrets that they are not like someone else, or to envy others who have gifts or advantages denied to them. Instead of setting about to discover and exercise the distinctive talents which have been entrusted to them, they endeavor to reproduce some human model. Such an attitude is a virtual denial of a personal plan for each life. The circumstances of each life are not accidental, but are designed by an all-wise Father who knows how best each can glorify Him and achieve the highest in life. When you recognize that God has fitted you for some specific task in some special sphere in which your powers will find their fullest and most harmonious exercise, then obedience to His leading will not be difficult.

Where this is understood, no detail of life is unimportant. Life becomes one long and romantic voyage of discovery. Had Philip delayed for one hour when God summoned him to go down to the desert, arguing with some justification that he was indispensable to the great revival movement in Samaria, his path would never have

crossed that of the Chancellor of the Ethiopian Ex-
chequer, and Ethiopia would have missed its early opportunity of hearing the gospel. Everything hinged on
his prompt and unquestioning obedience to the voice of
God's guiding Spirit. God's plan is not only individual,
but it is carefully timed.

## GUIDANCE IS CONDITIONAL

Few spiritual exercises are a greater test of our caliber
and maturity than the securing of divine guidance.

*Meekness* is one indispensable requisite. Self-will and
self-assertion effectively shut the door upon guidance.
"The meek will he guide in judgment" is the promise
(Ps 25:9). The meek person has a preference for the
will of God. Our Lord laid down an eternal principle
which applies equally to the guidance of the life and
guidance into truth when He said, "If any man willeth
to do his will he shall know" (Jn 7:17, ASV).

The prophet Balaam is a warning beacon to those who
profess to seek guidance while they are inwardly unwilling to conform to the revealed will of God. Instead of
having "his affections detached and his will fluid," his
eye was all the time fixed on the promised money. He
"loved the wages of unrighteousness" (2 Pe 2:15). Not
content with the divine refusal of permission to curse
Israel at the behest of King Balak, he plagued God until
He lifted the restraint. Had God changed His mind?
Not for a moment. But in view of Balaam's willful insistence, He said in effect, "Very well, if you *will,* you
*shall,*" and a disastrous decision it proved for Balaam.
The clearly expressed *directive* will of God was that he
should not go. The *permissive* will of God was that he
could go, but it would be acting in disobedience and on
his own responsibility. The tragic outcome was of his

own doing. The same thing was true of Abraham's journey into Egypt and Jonah's ill-fated excursion to Tarshish.

When God has indicated His will, it is a dangerous procedure to continue toying in our imagination with our own preconceived plan, as though to induce Him to change His mind. It has been said that the difference between the directive and the permissive will of God is simply the difference between God's purpose and ours.

*Obedience* in the ordinary duties of life will qualify for the reception of direction when we meet life's great crises. "In all thy ways [the broad highways of life] acknowledge him, and he shall direct thy paths [the forking byways]." Personal preferences should be honestly surrendered and then we will experience that "the integrity of the upright shall guide them" (Pr 11:3).

Our spiritual maturity and discernment will have a bearing on the manner of our guidance. Outward signs such as Gideon's fleece, far from being evidence of superior spirituality, are in reality a concession to feeble faith. The pillar of cloud and fire, the Urim and Thummim and the lot belonged to the kindergarten experience of the nation of Israel. In the time of their maturity, guidance became personal through the indwelling Spirit.

## GUIDANCE IS METHODICAL

There are certain principles, observance of which will ensure the knowledge of the will of God.

### GOD'S GUIDANCE WILL NEVER CONTRADICT HIS WORD

Where there is a clear statement in the Scriptures concerning the matter on which guidance is desired, no further guidance need be sought. God has already revealed His will. Any seeming guidance which is con-

trary to Scripture is palpably spurious. "To the law and
to the testimony: if they speak not according to this
word, it is because there is no light in them" (Is 8:20).

Dr. R A. Torrey wrote,

> We obtain guidance by taking the verse of Scrip-
> ture in the connection in which it is found in the
> Bible and interpreting it, as led by the Holy Spirit, in
> its context as found in the Bible. If the text suggested,
> taken in its real meaning as determined by the lan-
> guage used and by the context applies to your posi-
> tion, it is of course a message from God. If it has to
> be distorted from its proper meaning, it is no evidence
> that it is guidance from God.

There are times when a Scripture statement fairly
leaps at one from the page and is illumined by the Holy
Spirit as being clearly applicable to the situation under
review. In such cases, provided in its context it can
reasonably bear the suggested interpretation, it can be
confidently accepted as being an indication of the will
of God.

GOD'S SPIRIT WILL ALWAYS WITNESS TO GOD'S PLAN

"As many as are led by the Spirit of God, they are the
sons of God" (Ro 8:14). The Holy Spirit guides us by
quickening our discernment and enlightening our judgment, not by superseding it. In the classic passage re-
lating to the Spirit's guidance in perplexing circumstances, it is recounted that, after being "forbidden" and
"suffered not" to pursue their own plan, Paul and his
companions assuredly gathered that the Lord had called
them to preach the gospel in Macedonia (Ac 16:10).
An examination of the surrounding circumstances, however, shows that it was anything but a sudden decision.

It was a clear conviction resulting from much prayer, heart exercise and matured thought.

John Wesley claimed that God usually guided him by presenting reasons to his mind for acting in a certain way. It is for us to glean all the information available, and then to carefully weigh up the pros and cons before coming to a decision. As we pray, the Holy Spirit will impart a steadily deepening conviction that a certain course is the will of God. Those who are seeking guidance concerning a mission field, or some other sphere of Christian service, are less likely to receive some spectacular revelation of the place of God's choice than they are to receive a conviction which deepens as they pray.

## OUTWARD CIRCUMSTANCES WILL CONFIRM THE INWARD CONVICTION

When we are acting in line with God's will, surrounding circumstances will fall out accordingly. Gates of iron will open of their own accord. Insurmountable obstacles will melt away at the shout of faith. There will be complete harmony between the written Word, the witnessing Spirit and the providential circumstances.

But circumstances need testing. The favorable south wind (Ac 27), as Paul well knew, was unseasonable, and prudence would have counseled delay. Yielding to the lure of apparently good weather resulted in shipwreck. We dare not flout the warnings of common sense and experience simply because circumstances appear propitious.

In Jonah's flight to Tarshish, there was a discrepancy between God's word and his circumstances. In the case of the deception of the Gibeonites (Jos 9:14), Joshua acted on strong circumstantial evidence without waiting for the witnessing voice of the Spirit. His folly lay in that he "asked not counsel at the mouth of the LORD," but trusted in his own shrewdness. Divine guidance is not by the Spirit apart from the Word, or by the Word apart from the Spirit.

## GOD'S GUIDANCE WILL NOT VIOLATE CERTAIN PRINCIPLES

God's guidance will not violate an instructed conscience, common sense or the established proprieties of life. Nor will it lead one to neglect the plain duties of life. A mother whose sick child is dependent on her will not need to seek further guidance as to her sphere of service for the time being. Any guidance which would lead to eccentric action is at once suspect. Divine guidance manifests itself in Christian sanity.

## ADVICE OF QUALIFIED FRIENDS SHOULD BE SOUGHT

An independent opinion may throw a flood of light on the situation and elicit facts which we ourselves might easily have overlooked. We should not consult only those who we think would be favorable to the course of action which we would most like to follow. The views of those who might oppose such a course could be a valuable cross-check.

> Trust not thyself, but thy defects to know;
> Make use of every friend, *and every foe.*

If our plan is of God, opposition will not quench our zeal but will only serve to strengthen our conviction. But we should never allow others, however much we respect their counsel, to make our decisions for us. It is our future which is involved, and we must take the responsibility.

## GUIDANCE REQUIRES SAFEGUARDS

We must beware of claiming infallibility, as this will inevitably foster spiritual pride and unteachableness. Such expressions as, "The Lord told me to do so-and-so," or "The Lord revealed this to me" should be avoided. If it is true, the outcome will demonstrate that God did indeed tell us.

Even a direct answer to prayer, if our wills are biased in a certain direction, does not necessarily *by itself* indicate the divine approval. "He gave them their request; but sent leanness into their soul" (Ps 106:15) is a pertinent and solemn warning in this connection. Such guidance must be tested.

If disappointment, trouble, frustration or failure have influenced our decision, we should be doubly careful before acting on it. Had Paul and Silas allowed their reception in Philippi to sway them in their guidance, Europe might still have been without the gospel.

We should never be ashamed to own that we have mistaken our guidance if subsequent events prove that we have made a wrong turn. It would be dishonoring to God to persist in attributing to Him a course of action which does not have on it the seal of His approval. At best, the best of us is fallible. There is no sin in making a mistake when one has sincerely sought to do God's will.

The Bible should not be treated as a book of magic by adopting the "lucky dip" method. This is dishonoring both to the Bible and to one's own intelligence. The Bible is a reasonable book which will yield its secrets to the man who diligently seeks to hear the voice of God in it.

The voice of prejudice should not be confused with the voice of God. This is more frequently done than we

might think. In his zeal in persecuting the church, Paul
was convinced he was obeying the voice of God. Instead,
he was blinded by his own prejudice. Not until he was
struck down by the blaze of heavenly light did he discover his error.

We must beware of guidance which would lead to
hasty or ill-considered action. King Saul "forced himself" to offer a sacrifice in defiance of the command of
God. But his defiance cost him his kingdom. Time
spent in waiting is not lost. Even when the need for decision seems urgent, we should refuse to be hurried into
decision until we are perfectly sure of our guidance. In
uncertainty, the only safe course is to do nothing. It is
folly to act when the dove of peace has flown from the
heart. Most mistakes in guidance are made through a
failure to wait.

When the time for decision has come, there need be
no fear nor doubt. Where there is *submission,* a desire
only for the will of God, and *faith,* a confidence that the
Lord will guide as He has promised, there will be absolute rest of heart. Having consulted the Word of God
and spiritually wise friends, and having earnestly sought
the direction of the Holy Spirit in prayer, if circumstances and the inward peace of God unite to confirm
the decision reached, that decision can confidently be
accepted as the will of God. Paul's counsel is, "Let the
peace of God rule [arbitrate] in your hearts" (Col 3:15).

Having come to such a prayerful decision after having renounced personal preference and prejudice, there
is no reason to review or question your guidance. *Never
dig up in unbelief what you have sown in faith.* Begin
with the confidence that God will guide, and end with the
assurance that He has guided.

Do not lose heart in these days because of seemingly untoward things. God does not always rebuke the storm; but He does always reassure the storm-tossed believer. He does not always say, "Peace, be still"; but He does always say "Trust Me." God does not always let us see the end of the way, but He will give us light enough to take the next step in faith, in obedience, in surrender, in loyalty. And one day when the mists have rolled away, when the darkness has been dispelled, and the storm has spent itself, we shall find ourselves with Christ on the sunlit hill of Immanuel's Land. Then we shall know that this was the right road home, and shall sing with all the redeemed: "He hath done all things well."

J. STUART HOLDEN

# 2

# THE LESSON OF DIVINE SOVEREIGNTY

Blessed be the name of God for ever and ever: for wisdom and might are his: and he changeth the times and the seasons: he removeth kings, and setteth up kings: he giveth wisdom unto the wise, and knowledge to them that know understanding (Dan 2:20-21).

IN EVERY LIFE days come when faith has a hard battle to maintain its foothold. Even when we see and approve the purposes of God, His methods of achieving them sometimes seem baffling and mystifying. But nowhere in His Word does God undertake always to explain or justify Himself in His dealings with His children. He always leaves room for the exercise of faith. The fact is that there are some things in life which we are not meant to find out. There are some questions that a child asks which might permanently shadow his life if they were answered. In His mercy and love, there are some questions we ask which our Father does not answer. "There is a silence that is more precious than speech," wrote Dr. J. Stuart Holden. "There is a darkness that is fuller of heaven than is light; there is a storm that is better than calm; for it blows away the selfishness and pride and every hateful thing from our lives, and braces our courage and faith."

If we are to enjoy peace and serenity in the fever of a world in political and social revolution, we must strengthen our grip on the neglected but steadying fact of the sovereignty of God.

## THE SOVEREIGNTY OF GOD

When King Nebuchadnezzar's understanding returned to him after the judgment of God had deprived him of his reason, he uttered a remarkable statement concerning the nature and extent of the sovereignty of God which is in accordance with the tenor of Scripture: "He doeth according to his will in the army of heaven, and among the inhabitants of the earth: and none can stay his hand, or say unto him, What doest thou?" (Dan 4:35).

God is no indulgent Father who gives His children whatever they desire whenever they want it, irrespective of moral and spiritual considerations. God is indeed our Father in heaven, but He is also sovereign King and moral Governor of the universe. He treats the peoples of the earth as responsible moral beings, as freewill agents, not as robots. If they choose sin, He does not violate their freewill but allows their sin to take its normal course and to have its natural and inevitable fruitage. The grim tragedies enacted in so many parts of the contemporary world are but the operation of the inexorable law: "Whatsoever a man [or nation] soweth, that shall he also reap" (Gal 6:7). The nations of the world have sown the wind and are reaping the whirlwind, and the innocent are suffering with the guilty.

Men ignore and blaspheme God, flout His laws, desecrate His day, despise His church and reject His Son— and then have the effrontery to blame Him for the outworking of their sin. In the rise and progress of Communism, God is writing in letters of fire the bitter lesson that sin brings suffering and bloodshed to the nations, even as it brought suffering and the shedding of blood to Him who bore its penalty on Calvary.

SOVEREIGNTY AND PATERNITY

The parable of the potter is calculated to bring comfort to the scholar in this school of God. "Cannot I do with you as this potter?" He asked of Israel (Jer 18:6). He claimed to have the same absolute power over the nation as the potter exercised over the clay. The simile is harsh and cruel until it is interpreted by another scripture: "But now, O LORD, thou art our father; we are the clay and thou our potter" (Is 64:8). The one who is the Potter is also our Father. While it is absolute, His sovereignty can never clash with His paternity. Because the hand which molds the clay is nail-pierced, we can have unbounded confidence that every act which God in His sovereignty performs or permits, however inscrutable to us, is always in our highest interests. With our Lord we can believe that the will of our Father is "perfect love expressed in the terms of perfect wisdom." It is here that our faith must become operative.

BESTOWAL AND WITHDRAWAL

To the believing heart, God's hand is seen as clearly in what He withdraws from life as in what He bestows. And yet, how much more readily we are prepared to recognize His agency in the latter than in the former. In this our attitude contrasts strongly with that of Job, although he lived in the twilight days of divine self-disclosure, while we enjoy the full revelation of God in Christ.

After a period of unclouded prosperity, Job was suddenly overwhelmed by a veritable tornado of trouble.

Tragedy succeeded tragedy. In quick succession he was bereft of flocks and herds, home, servants, sons and daughters. He was stunned by these unexpected visitations, but it is in circumstances such as these that the true quality of a man's faith is seen. How did he react? Did he blame God, question His love, and flounce out of His presence? No, indeed. He gave sublime expression to his faith:

> The LORD gave, and the LORD hath taken away; blessed be the name of the LORD. Shall we receive good at the hand of God, and shall we not receive evil? Though he slay me, yet will I trust in him" (Job 1:21; 2:10; 13:15).

These were words, not of callous fatalism but of triumphant faith. Job knew his God. He recognized that the sovereign God who had given also had a perfect right to take away. Although through much heart-searching he could assign no reason for such calamities (for was he not conscious of his own integrity?), without premeditation he had his answer ready and bowed submissively to the sovereign will of God. This is a lesson which we who live in the full blaze of gospel light should master too.

It was the author's privilege on one occasion to share the sadness of parting, with a loved friend. When she learned that the father of her three young children would never return to their home, we accompanied her from the hospital. In the car we mingled our tears as we poured out our hearts to God. Suddenly a great calm came to the tormented heart and the tears were stanched. Then followed an unforgettable prayer. "O Lord, I know that Thou art going to take my loved one to Thyself. But before Thou dost take him, I give him back to

Thee who didst give him to me. I thank Thee for the happy years we have spent together, and in the dark days to come, I will never ask Thee, 'Why?' " The years of a fragrant testimony which have followed have demonstrated that the prayer was more than empty words.

There are many unsolved mysteries in God's providences. Why did He give Peter three thousand souls while faithful Stephen received three thousand stones? Why did He grant deliverance to Peter while the equally devoted James was beheaded? It was not that one was more deserving than the other. We must await the dawning of the perfect day for the answer to all our questions. "At best we can see only parts of His ways and understand only segments of the whole circle of His truth." It is here that the test of faith comes in. We may enjoy the security of the character and integrity of our Lord who said, "What I do thou knowest not now; but thou shalt know hereafter" (Jn 13:7).

Some visitors to a deaf and dumb school were invited to write on the blackboard any question they desired the children to answer. One person was sufficiently thoughtless or callous to ask, "Why did God make you deaf and dumb, while He gave other children speech and hearing?" There was tense silence for a few moments and tears glistened in the eyes of some of the children. Then one boy took the chalk and wrote this sublime answer. "Even so, Father, for so it seemed good in Thy sight." This child had learned a deep lesson concerning the unexplainable dealings of the Lord which many older Christians have failed to master: "Blessed is he, whosoever shall not be offended in me" (Mt 11:6).

When with Job we can bow our heads and say, "Blessed be the name of the Lord," we have progressed no little distance along the pathway of faith toward spiritual maturity. Although as yet His actions may seem to us mysterious and mystifying, from the battlements of Immanuel's land we shall see and approve the wisdom of Him whose way is perfect.

Another mystifying element in the divine providences is the slowness of God.

## THE SLOWNESS OF GOD

We are always in a hurry to have our desires granted, our prayers answered. But God refuses to be stampeded into premature action. Our impatience is the outcome of an undisciplined spirit, or an imperfect knowledge of all the facts and an inadequate realization of their full implications. God's seeming slowness is only the reaction of full knowledge and perfect control of every contingency that might arise.

In time of war, bleeding hearts cry, "God could bring all this slaughter and bloodshed to an end in a moment. Why does He wait? Why does He not intervene?"

Why not! Certainly not because He is *physically* unable, or that He is unwilling to do so. The only answer is that He is *morally* unable to do so. We must recognize that there are things which are moral and spiritual impossibilities to God. He cannot lie. He cannot deny Himself. He cannot save a sinful man apart from repentance and faith. God does not glory in war and bloodshed, and He will intervene when it is morally right to do so. When He sees a nation bow in humiliation and confession of its national sins, it becomes possible and right for Him to intervene. When wicked Nineveh publicly expressed its repentance, God immediately responded by lifting the judgment. It is not God who is too slow, but man who is too sinful.

How slow God sometimes seems in granting the answer to our prayers! Months and even years go by and yet there is no apparent response. George Müller prayed for more than sixty years for the salvation of two men. The answer came in the case of one of the men just before Müller's death and the other shortly after. What a long, drawn-out test of faith this was, but how wonderful an education in the prayer of faith it proved to the one who prayed.

Sometimes God is slow in granting the answer to our prayers in order that we may learn lessons we could master in no other way. We pray for the salvation or the sanctification of our children, and the answer sometimes seems more remote than ever. But God has not forgotten His promises. It is for us to maintain the attitude of confident faith as exemplified by Abraham of whom it is written, "He relied on the word of God. . . . With undaunted faith he looked at the facts . . . he refused to allow any distrust of a definite pronouncement of God to make him waver. He drew strength from his faith, and . . . remained absolutely convinced that God was able to implement his own promise" (Ro 4:19-21, Phillips).

> Unanswered yet, the prayer your lips have pleaded
> In agony of heart these many years?
> Does faith begin to fail? Is hope departing?
> And think you all in vain those falling tears?
> Say not the Father hath not heard your prayer,
> You shall have your desire—sometime, somewhere.

Once again the apparent slowness of God to act when to us action seems urgent and imperative unless all is to be lost, can be a great challenge to our faith. But both history and experience unite to teach that He will move at exactly the right moment. His providential care is always in exercise on behalf of His children. We can afford to quietly commit, trust and rest.

In time of stress or sorrow, one of the most perplexing problems is the silence of God.

## THE SILENCE OF GOD

It was Carlyle who complained in an hour of deep distress, that the worst of all was that God did nothing. But He was wrong. Although He stands amid the shadows and does not disclose His presence and concern, His unerring hand never loses hold of the reins.

In his perplexity Isaiah plaintively cried, "Verily thou art a God that hidest thyself" (45:15). He failed to discern in the bewildering events that were happening around him, any evidence of the activity of God. To his cry of distress there came no answering voice from heaven.

> Thrice blest is he to whom is given
> The instinct that can tell
> That God is on the field, when He
> Is most invisible.
>
> FABER

This is one of the sublime activities of faith. When Christ ascended on high, angelic messengers promised His return and the early Christians cherished the hope of His speedy advent. Their common greeting in the streets was, "Maranatha, the Lord is coming." But the trump and the voice of the archangel are still silent, although two millenniums have elapsed. Scoffers both within and without the church are saying, "Where is the promise of His coming?" Yet the silence remains unbroken. Peter reveals one reason for His silence—"The Lord is not slack concerning his promise . . . but is long-suffering . . . not willing that any should perish" (2 Pe 3:9).

John the Baptist was in prison for Christ's sake. He had exchanged the open spaces of the desert for the stifling atmosphere of an eastern dungeon. But although Jesus was not very far away, He did not visit him, or even send a message of appreciation and consolation. At last John could endure his tormenting doubts no longer. He dispatched his disciples to Jesus with the poignant question, "Art Thou he that should come, or do we look for another?" Even this question elicited no direct answer. But Jesus commissioned the messengers to return to John with a report of the miracles they had seen—miracles which authenticated His claim to Messiahship—and He added this postscript, "Blessed is he, whosoever shall find no occasion of stumbling in me" (Mt 11:6). Even though John might find His silence unreasonable and inexplicable, true blessedness would come to him as he trusted his Master even in the darkness.

The home in Bethany was a loved and relaxing rendezvous of the Lord and no guest was more welcome than He. The warmth of love of Mary and Martha and Lazarus was heartily reciprocated by their Guest. Now Lazarus had fallen seriously ill. The sisters, confident of His ability to help and heal, immediately sent a message to Jesus. He would surely hasten to their side in their hour of need. But He did not come. Their anguished eyes saw the pallor of death steal over the loved face. The record reads strangely, "When he had heard that he [Lazarus] was sick, he abode two days still in the same place where he was" (Jn 11:6). What a strange way of demonstrating His love! He even said to His disciples, "I am glad for your sakes that I was not there."

When at length Jesus did come, Lazarus had been dead four days and Martha and Mary reproached Him in identical words: "Lord, if thou hadst been here, my brother had not died." They had found no satisfying answer to His strange silence and neglect. Of His genuine sympathy there could be no doubt, for a short while later we read, "Jesus wept." But He had greater ends in view. He did not shun permitting them to suffer present sorrow, because only thus could they see the glory of God. He was glad He had not come at their call, not for His own sake, but for theirs. The two sisters and the disciples had a new and more glorious Lord after the raising of Lazarus. Henceforth they knew Him as "the resurrection and the Life." From the vantage point of "afterward," they were able to rejoice in the love which had not responded to their plea.

"The wonderful thing about the Lord is that He is content to be misunderstood by His children in the meantime," wrote Dr. J. Stuart Holden. "Thou knowest not now until the time is fully ripe, but thou shalt know hereafter. The years justify a great deal of what we vainly try to interpret in the present. Time is God's ally, and the future is all on God's side. Time solves most of our problems."

We must accept it that in all His dealings the sovereign Lord has in view the ultimate benefit of His people, rather than their present comfort. His silence may be inexplicable to human reason, but it can be acceptable to the humble faith which says, "Even so, Father, for so it seemed good in thy sight" (Mt 11:26).

During the Japanese war in China, a lame Chinese

Christian woman limped thirteen miles to attend the
annual meetings of the church. Every step had hurt
and her sore eyes were freshly inflamed by the dust-
laden wind. "Unloosening her heart" a bit she said,
"During this last year my home has been twice burnt
and nothing has been saved. Four of my six relatives
there have died, including my brother who was branded
with hot irons. My daughter-in-law was shot through
the lungs before my eyes, and my only little grandson
died from exposure. *Yet* will I not let go of Jesus Christ.
I will not blame Him."

Last, let us reflect on the stability of God.

## THE STABILITY OF GOD

"I wonder if God is as good and loving as we have
been led to believe?" Coming as these words did from
the lips of a lifelong church member, they compel the
conclusion that this failure of faith in the midst of perplexity is by no means an isolated one.

It is true that all around us is in a state of flux. The
whole world senses that it stands in an unprecedented
crisis. International law is no longer respected. National
boundaries change overnight. Cherished institutions
have crashed in ruins. High ideals have been raped by
unscrupulous leaders. And what of God? Has He
changed? There is solid ground on which to plant the
feet of our faith.

> I am the LORD, I change not; therefore ye sons of
> Jacob are not consumed (Mal 3:6).
> Jesus Christ the same yesterday, and to day, and
> for ever (Heb 13:8).

> I change, He changes not,
> My joy still ebbs and flows,

> But peace with God remains the same,
> No change Jehovah knows.

The hand that controls the universe is the very hand that was pierced for us on the cross. The attitude of Him who there suffered the supreme indignity for us has suffered no change. His heart is the same today as when He wept at the grave of Lazarus or over doomed Jerusalem. *He has not changed.* He cannot act in any way inconsistent with His character as the Truth. His activities among His people are always in keeping with His unchanging nature, and always according to the pulsations of His loving heart!

There are some friends whom we know intimately, whose friendship has been so tested and proved that no matter what they did, even if it bore every appearance of being an unfriendly act, we would believe in them without reserve. We are maturing spiritually when our trust in God has advanced sufficiently far as to enable us to say of Him, "I know Him so well that no matter what He does, I still trust His unchanging love."

This is the attitude that brings true rest of heart and repose of mind, for in the final analysis true security is based on the stability of God.

If I speak with the tongues of the angels above, or the tongues of the seers, but am lacking in love, my words are all hollow, nor will they surpass the clatter of cymbals, the clanging of brass. If I see as a prophet and know as a sage and read the occult as an obvious page, and the might of my faith can a mountain remove, with it all I am nothing if I have not love. If I give to the poor all the wealth I have earned, and if as a martyr my body is burned, and love does not move to the gift or the pain, they profit me nothing, my bounties are vain. Love suffereth long, and is endlessly kind; Love envieth not nor is haughty in mind; Love never is harsh; love seeks not her own; and a grudge and revenge to love are unknown. Love praises no evil, is true as the day; love heareth, believeth, and hopeth for aye. Though knowledge may cease, and though prophecies pale, love never, no never, no never shall fail. Now ever abideth the faith of the free, and high hope, and love, these dominant three; but greatest and happiest, soaring above all glories, all joys, and all powers is love.

AMOS R. WELLS

34

# 3

## THE LESSON OF LOVE

Love suffereth long, and is kind; love vaunteth not itself, is not puffed up, doth not behave itself unseemly, seeketh not its own, is not provoked, taketh not account of evil; rejoiceth not in unrighteousness, but rejoiceth with the truth; beareth all things, believeth all things, hopeth all things, endureth all things. Love never faileth (1 Co 13:4-8, ASV).

THE PREEMINENT PLACE accorded to love is a distinctive feature of Christianity. In no other religion is love exalted as the primary virtue. The life which does not have love as its mainspring cannot be said to be truly Christian. The Lord of love said, "By this [love] shall all men know that ye are my disciples" (Jn 13:35), for love is His emblem.

> Beloved, let us love: for they who love,
> They only, are His sons, born from above.

Paul's hymn of love is at once the most beautiful and the most humbling paragraph in the whole Bible. No thoughtful reader can emerge from the chapter the same as he entered it. Its dazzling light ruthlessly exposes motives, analyzes character and tests service. God's standard for the believer's life is set, not by the two tables of the law, but by the perfect life of Him who was the incarnation of love.

No more beautiful epitome of His blameless life and character can be found than in this choice idyll. If the chapter is read, substituting "Christ" for "charity," it will be found that every statement is matched and fulfilled in His peerless character. The substitution of one's own name for "charity" affords a humbling contrast.

> I am always longsuffering and kind; I am never envious; I am never puffed up; I never behave myself unseemly, I never seek my own, I am never provoked, I never think evil; I never rejoice in iniquity but I always rejoice in the truth; I bear all things, I believe all things, I hope all things, I endure all things. I never fail.

An honest self-appraisal in the light of this holy ideal must produce conviction and contrition in the heart of any spiritually sensitve Christian and cause him to pray with intense longing:

> Gracious Spirit, Holy Ghost,
> Taught by Thee we covet most,
> Of Thy gifts at Pentecost,
>    Holy, heavenly love.

## THE PREEMINENCE OF LOVE (vv. 1-3)

One writer claims that this chapter is probably the most wonderful parenthesis in the Bible, an inspiring hymn relieving the tension of a delicate discussion, a cooling influence when feelings were likely to be growing heated.

On either side of it there is the noise of controversy, a striking contrast to its own beauty and tranquillity. There is no room for controversy here, no room for argument. Every statement is categorical. The supremacy of love is axiomatic in the Christian life. It was the daily habit of the saintly Andrew Murray to read this chapter on his knees. Small wonder then that his life was so impregnated with the Spirit of Christ and that his fragrant ministry persists the world around half a century after his death.

In the paragraph under consideration love is contrasted with several of the most prized charismatic gifts of the richly endowed Corinthian church. Paul admits that they came behind no other church in spiritual gifts (1 Co 1:7), but he warns them that no gift can compensate for the absence of love.

First, he indicates the supremacy of love *over the gift of tongues* (v. 1). The possession of the gift of ecstatic utterance or brilliant rhetoric or burning eloquence—of the Pentecostal enduement in its highest form, if love is lacking, is no more attractive than the brassy clanging of a dissonant cymbal. The touchstone is not words of love on the lips, but outward evidence of love in the heart. We must obey the apostolic injunction to "covet earnestly the best gifts," but we must not neglect at the same time to cultivate the graces of the Spirit which impart to the gifts any true spiritual value. The Corinthians had a weakness for brilliance but Paul insists that *love is more than eloquence*.

Love is transcendent *over the gift of prophecy* (v. 2). The reference here is doubtless to inspired preaching, whether predictive or perceptive. Prophecy uniformly heads the list of charismatic gifts, and because of its power of edification in the church, Paul urges all to covet it. "And yet, I show you a more excellent way," the way of love, he writes. Many ardent fundamentalists neutralize their testimony to the truth by their unloving words and criticisms. Unlike their Master, they do not display the perfect balance between grace and

truth. Let us speak the truth by all means, but let it be
in love.

The power to unravel "all mysteries," the possession
of profound erudition, the ability to plumb and pro-
pound the deep things of God—all these count for nothing in the absence of love. As Matthew Henry put it,
"A clear and deep head is of no significance without a
benevolent and loving heart." *Love is more than knowledge.*

Love is supreme *over miracle-working faith* (v. 2).
No believer is disposed to minimize the value and importance of faith in every aspect of the Christian life,
least of all Paul. The vital part it plays cannot be over-
estimated, for "without faith it is impossible to please
God." But it should always be remembered that "faith
worketh by love" (Gal 5:6). If faith is out of proportion to love, her apparent success is failure. Even the
receiving of spectacular answers to prayer is no acceptable substitute for a love-filled life. We have often
prayed, "Lord, increase our faith," but someone has
suggested the addition of another petition, "Lord, increase our love, lest our faith be in vain." *Love is more
than faith.*

The superlative excellence of love *over heartless
charity* is emphasized (v. 3). Few activities secure the
commendation of men—and rightly so—more than philanthropy. Yet, "if I share out all my goods morsel by
morsel, but have not love, it profiteth me NOTHING,"
says Deissman. The purity of the motive determines
the quality of the action. Ananias emulated Barnabas
in making a munificent gift, but the unworthy motive
robbed the act of all spiritual value and rendered the
gift wholly unacceptable to God. We should closely
scrutinize the motive which prompts our philanthropy

lest love of display or desire for approbation displace love. *Love is more than philanthropy.*

*Love eclipses ostentatious martyrdom* (v. 3). Surely the highest pinnacle of human self-sacrifice is reached in martyrdom. What can a man give more than life itself? But Paul insists that even the sublime act of self-oblation could profit the martyr nothing if the motive of love were lacking. Archbishop H. C. Lees records that in Athens, the city where Paul saw the altar inscribed "To the Unknown God," he might also have seen the tomb of an Indian fakir, Zarmanochegas. It bore the epitaph: "Zarmanochegas, the Indian from Bargosa, according to the ancient customs of India, made himself immortal and lies here."

How did he make himself immortal? By burning himself publicly in the streets of Athens. These words were doubtless penned with such cases in view. The writer knew of those who, for the sake of ambition, or of personal glory rather than from love to God and man, would even seek martyrdom. How different was it with Stephen, whose martyrdom found its motive in flaming love in his Lord. And with Blandina, the slave girl who, "cherishing her love for Him, died an agonizing death." *Love is more than self-sacrifice.*

Herein lies the preeminence of love. "It transcends the way of splendid speech, of Scriptural scholarship, and of supreme sacrifice." The Master spoke with the tongue of men and of angels. He exercised the gift of prophecy, He understood all mysteries and all knowledge, He had all faith, He bestowed all His goods on others, He gave His body in martyrdom. Because love was the motive and source of all He did, His words and deeds are deathless and His life transcendently fruitful.

## THE PROPERTIES OF LOVE (vv. 4-7)

When Paul is talking about possible defects of character and service, with delicate tact he includes himself by employing the first person. But now that he is about to enumerate the excellences of love, he uses the third person. It is noteworthy that the properties of love set forth are mainly negative. Love is known better by what she can refrain from doing than from her manifold activities. First we notice her patience.

### LOVE'S PATIENCE

"Love suffereth long." It is not without significance that the forbearance of love comes first. It is not so much what love can do as how long love can suffer without breaking down, for it is long-suffering *with people* which is in view here. Love's severest tests come in the realm of our relations with our fellowmen. "Lord, how oft shall my brother sin against me and I forgive him? Till seven times?" Peter doubtless thought he was being very generous until he heard the Master's reply: "I say not unto thee, Until seven times: but, Until seventy times seven" (Mt 18:21-22).

Love does not balk at the first hurdle, she finishes the race. No matter how strong the provocation, she is never betrayed into ill-advised speech or precipitate action that will later be bitterly regretted. She knows how to hold her peace even amid gross injustice. Love's long-suffering found its crowning demonstration on the slopes of Mt. Calvary, where the supreme Sufferer, instead of calling down maledictions, prayed for His tormentors.

### LOVE'S BENEVOLENCE

"Love is kind." Kindness has been defined as a disposition to place oneself at the disposal of others, irrespective of their position or disposition. What a benediction kind people are in a cold and unsympathetic world. They are always on the lookout to be of service to someone else.

Lady Bartle Frere once requested a young guest to meet her husband at the railway station.

"But how shall I recognize him?" asked the young man. "I have never met him."

"Just look for a tall gentleman helping someone" was the response. "That will be my husband."

## LOVE'S GENEROSITY

"Love envieth not." Envy has an unenviable record. Was it not envy that staged the first murder? Was it not envy that hurried the Lord of glory along the road to the cross? Pilate "knew that for envy they had delivered him."

Love knows no envy of her more gifted sister, no jealousy of his more honored brother. She is generous and large-hearted toward rivals. The advancement or preferment of another does not cause chagrin but affords genuine joy. Was ever saint more devoid of envy than John the Baptist who alienated his congregation in favor of his Rival? Not every preacher urges his congregation to attend the church around the corner! We may test ourselves on this point by asking the question, Does the superiority or success of another, especially one in the same line of work as myself, stimulate my envy or my joy?

> These things are the sins I fain
> Would have Thee take away;
> Malice and cold disdain,
> Hot anger, sullen hate,

Scorn of the lowly, envy of the great,
And discontent that casts a shadow grey
On all the brightness of the common day.

HENRY VAN DYKE

## LOVE'S MODESTY

"Love vaunteth not itself," makes no parade, does not "show off," is not boastful or forward. The word here is the very word used by Cicero in speaking of a great oratorical effort before Pompey: "Good heavens, how I showed myself off before my new hearer, Pompey."

But true love assumes no airs, does not inordinately desire to be noticed or applauded. She can hear both the attainments or afflictions of others without seeking to eclipse them. She does not belittle others to increase her own stature. "Folk admire the peacock for the grandeur of his plumes, until they are driven away by the discordant tones of his voice." The peacock is the emblem of the boaster.

## LOVE'S HUMILITY

"Love is not puffed up," is not imprisoned in a sense of her own importance. Instead of courting adulation and advertisement, she delights in effacing herself, satisfied if thereby her Master's stature is increased and His interests advanced. Pride finds no place in her heart because she recognizes she has nothing which she has not received. Pride is essentially competitive in nature. C. S. Lewis points out that no one is proud because he is rich or clever or good-looking. He is proud because he is richer or cleverer or better-looking than someone else. It involves a comparison which always goes in favor of the one who makes it. This is the very antithesis of love.

LOVE'S COURTESY

"Love doth not behave itself unseemly," is always courteous and becoming in demeanor. Love *cannot* be rude; it is contrary to her nature. Being always solicitous for the comfort and sensitive to the feelings of others, she never forgets her manners. To snub another, to wither with a word or freeze with a look would be entirely out of character. Love does not violate the proprieties of life or the courtesies of speech. Sarcasm is unknown to love, for it is always calculated to hurt and is therefore essentially unloving. Courtesy is not merely a matter of birth; it is a matter of the spirit and is innate in those who love. "What breeding does by training, love does by instinct."

It is told of Louis XIV of France that on one occasion he was recounting a story before his courtiers in Versailles, when suddenly he ended it very poorly. A few minutes later a prince left the room. The king then said, "You must have noticed how lamely my story ended. I forgot that it reflected on an ancestor of the prince who has just left the room and I thought it better to spoil a good story than to distress a good man."

LOVE'S SELFLESSNESS

"Love seeketh not her own." Here surely is a counsel of perfection for we seek our own as naturally as we breathe air.

In copying this chapter, a scribe who was working on the Vatican manuscript paused in astonishment at this amazing sentence. He felt sure there must be a mistake somewhere and that what the text really meant was, "Love seeketh not what is *not* her own," so he inserted the extra "not." He could not understand the truly selfless character of love. It was an exotic which he had never seen blooming in the lives with which he had had contact. It is characteristic of true love that it is not solicitous of its own happiness.

"For all seek their own, not the things which are Jesus Christ's," mourned Paul (Phil 2:21). "I seek not mine own," affirmed the Son of God (Jn 5:20). What is the object of our pursuit? Do we cling tenaciously to our own rights, or do we surrender them in the interests of the one who is the object of our love? The apostle had earned the right to speak of selflessness. His testimony was, "Nevertheless we have not exercised this right, but suffer all things, lest we should hinder the gospel." "Let no man seek his own, but every man another's good."

## LOVE'S SELF-CONTROL

"Love is not provoked." For some inexplicable reason—probably a sop to the weakness of human nature —the Authorized Version translates the clause, "Love is not easily provoked." But the word "easily" just is not there. The truth is that love *never* gives way to provocation, exasperation or irritation. Nor is she touchy and ready to imagine a slight.

"I think the crowning glory of our Lord," wrote Dr. W. Y. Fullerton, "was that He was never impatient once. He was not only sinless as we count sinlessness, but amid the rush of things, with a tired mind and a restless crowd, He was never impatient."

Provocation and irritation are the outward evidence of an inner breakdown of love. If the people in our home fear what reception they will receive from us when they come down to breakfast, it is because love is lacking.

## LOVE'S MAGNANIMITY

"Love thinketh no evil." She does not keep an account of the wrongs she has suffered. She is a poor mathematician. She is always ready to impute a worthy motive, always giving the higher motive the benefit of the doubt.

Archbishop Cranmer, a martyr, was a notable example of this quality of love. Of him it was said, "Do the Archbishop a displeasure, and you will ever have him as your friend." In his last message he said, "I had never any greater pleasure in all my life than to forget and forgive injuries and to show kindness to them that sought evil to me." Abraham Lincoln was of similar disposition. He had a short memory for injuries, but never forgot a kindness.

## LOVE'S SINCERITY

"Love rejoiceth not in iniquity but rejoiceth in the truth." Moffatt helpfully renders it, "Love is never gladdened when another goes wrong. She is always gladdened by goodness." She finds no pleasure even in the fall of an enemy, nor is she mean enough to feel herself better because others have proved themselves worse. Instead, she mourns over iniquity. She takes no pleasure in being the conveyer of an evil tale.

## LOVE'S SILENCE

"Love beareth [covereth] all things." One rendering is "Love knows how to be silent." Another, "Love is always slow to expose." Both of these translations bring out the idea behind the word "beareth." Like her Lord, when love is reviled, she reviles not again, but takes a delight in concealing the faults of others.

When the artist engaged by Alexander the Great

drew his portrait, he made the shadow of his hand cover the scar on his brow. Love is ingenious in devising ways of throwing a mantle of silence over the faults of others.

### LOVE'S TRUST

"Love believeth all things." Love is not gullible but she is guileless and unsuspicious. She puts the best construction on every ambiguous action. Love is credulous where the object of affection is concerned, and refuses to credit evil except after the most exhaustive inquiry and on unmistakable evidence.

Dr. A. B. Simpson suggests that here is the secret of loving people whom we do not even like. Love can believe for them what it does not see; can clothe them with qualities they do not possess; and then can trust God to make them true, and can treat them as if true. Like God, she will "not see iniquity in Jacob, nor perverseness in Israel." She steadfastly refuses to believe evil of others and persists in believing the good.

### LOVE'S OPTIMISM

"Love hopeth all things," for she is absolutely undiscourageable. Even when there appears to be no reasonable basis for hope, in her sublime optimism love hopes on. She despairs of no one. Nothing taxes the love of the Christian worker more than the repeated falls and betrayals of confidence of one he is trying to help. It is here that love comes in, for she is perennially sanguine.

### LOVE'S FORTITUDE

"Love endureth all things." It is told of Lord Palmerston that on one occasion he was discussing the merits of the armies of Europe with a distinguished Frenchman who said, "You know, Palmerston, I think the French soldiers are the bravest in the world." "I cannot make the same claim for the British soldier," replied Palmerston. "I think there are other soldiers just as brave as the Britisher, but the British soldier is brave a quarter of an hour longer than any other soldier."

It was in this quality that the love of Christ shone so brilliantly. He "endured such contradiction of sinners against himself" and "endured the cross, despising the shame" (Heb 12:3, 2).

To summarize:

> When hurt, love bears;
> When despised, she believes;
> When disappointed, she hopes;
> When persecuted, she endures.

### THE PERMANENCE OF LOVE (vv. 8-13)

"Love never faileth." We have reached the climax. Love is like her Lord who, "having loved his own which were in the world, loved them unto the end." As the original word used here suggests, love's flower petals never fall, for she is a perennial. All else is transient but love knows neither diminution nor decline.

The triad of gifts—prophecy, tongues, knowledge—will vanish; the triad of graces will remain. "And now abideth faith, hope and love, but the greatest of these is love." Of these three abiding graces, love enjoys the place of preeminence. It is the crown of all, inimitable and indestructible.

### THE PURSUIT OF LOVE

"Follow after love." This love does not become ours as a matter of course. We are to pursue it as earnestly as the hunter pursues his quarry or the athlete his sport. Our pursuit is to be both eager and persevering.

If gifts without love are worthless; if love is the fairest flower in the garden of the soul; if love is the most abiding of all graces, then these are surely adequate reasons to spur us on in pursuit of her.

A preacher was walking along a street in the university town of Cambridge, when he passed a florist's windows. One was filled with bulbs and seeds. It was neither pretty nor attractive so he passed it with a mere glance. The other window was filled with blossoms of great beauty—crocuses, hyacinths, tulips. He was immediately arrested, and as he admired the flowers he greatly desired to possess the unlovely bulbs and seeds which enshrined such beauty and fragrance.

As we admire the beauty and breathe the fragrance emanating from the King of love, do we not yearn to give Him such undisputed sway in our hearts that He will be able to reproduce in our lives His own aroma and attractiveness?

The great need of which Christians everywhere are conscious, is that of power. Wherever a number of believers gather together for prayer, this is usually the burden of their cry. The need is so patent and universal as not to require any insistence or emphasis, for it is on all hands attested by fruitlessness of life and by barrenness of service. The fact is that despite the promises of God, the majority of His people are living lives which are so powerless and ineffective as to be a standing contradiction of the ideals and inducements of His Word.

In order to know the fullest possible measure of power for service there must be a complete separation unto the divine purpose for which power is bestowed. God does not invest a man with power for any other work than that of the kingdom, and no man who does not renounce all forms of leadership other than spiritual can ever know the enduement of a personal Pentecost. Politics, literature, the fine arts, intellectual pursuits, have each their own legitimate sphere, but the power of the Holy Ghost is never bestowed to make a man a worker or a leader in these things. Only for the glory of Christ in the salvation of souls can the holy enduement be sought with any certainty of realization, and herein is the explanation of the failure of much desire and many prayers.

J. STUART HOLDEN

# 4

# THE LESSON OF POWER

I am full of power by the spirit of the LORD (Mic 3:8).

THE DISTINGUISHING FEATURES of Pentecostal Christianity were the great power and effectiveness of its witness. The outstanding characteristics of twentieth century Christianity, on the contrary, are impotence and ineffectiveness in witness. The reason for this discrepancy is not hard to trace. In both pulpit and pew there tends to be a practical ignoring of the Holy Spirit who mediates the power of the risen Christ. Why did the ignorant and unlearned men of the early church succeed in turning the world upside down? Because they discovered and tapped the secret of spiritual power—a secret open to all.

## LONGINGS FOR POWER

We live in a power-hungry and power-conscious age. Every heart, whether regenerate or unregenerate, craves for power in one form or another. With the sincere Christian there is an inarticulate but ardent longing for power for holy living and successful service. The motives behind this longing may be selfish in part, but the genuine desire is there. Power can be divine or it can be devilish. When wielded by a Hitler or a Stalin it can be ruthless and tyrannical because it is divorced from morality, and nothing can be more dangerous than power of this kind. But nothing can be more beneficent than a power which is motivated by selfless love.

Jonathan Goforth was one of the most honored revivalists of this century. The ardor of his longing for spiritual power can be judged by his own words: "Restless, discontented, I was led to a more intensive study of the Scripture. Every passage that had any bearing on the price of, or the road to, the accession of power became life and breath to me. . . . So much did it become an obsession with me that my wife began to fear my mind would not stand it."

God could not and did not disappoint this passionate yearning, and Goforth lived to see thousands of people moved by the Spirit of God as corn before the wind. If we covet spiritual power we must be willing to pay the price entailed.

## LACK OF POWER

Socrates maintained that his greatest work was "to bring men from ignorance unconscious to ignorance conscious." So it may be said that it is the work of the Spirit of God to bring us from impotence unconscious to impotence conscious. Only then can He create in us a yearning for spiritual effectiveness. Our impotence is patent enough to the people around us. We are surrounded by hordes of young men and women who are entirely beyond the reach of the church. There is no point of contact. Our beaches and streets are thronged with multitudes for whom spiritual things have no meaning and Christ has no relevance, and we seem powerless to influence them toward God. We preach, but how many turn to Him in true repentance and faith? The truth is, the church is largely powerless to arrest the headlong downward drift of humanity. Her voice is muffled by her compromises and infidelities. A powerless church is a reproach to Christ, and all of its organization and equipment is, to a great extent, futile. On the other hand, a church in which the Holy Spirit is honored, as in the church at Antioch, exerts an incalculable influence on its own generation. So powerful was the witness of that church that one person in two in the great city of Antioch was reputed to be a Christian.

The disciples had not descended from their exalted experience on the Mount of Transfiguration before they were confronted with the distraught father of a demon-possessed lad. Recounting what had happened, the father said in distressed surprise, "I spake to thy disciples that they should cast him out; *and they could not*" (Mk 9:18). Later, when they had the Lord to themselves, the disciples ventured to ask Him, "Why could not we cast him out?" Their impotence was complete and tragic, but the saving feature was that it was conscious. They were not content to remain impotent. Their powerlessness was conscious and confessed, and the Lord was able to meet them in their need. His answer disclosed the cause. By himself man cannot rise above the level of the human any more than water can rise above its own level. For a superhuman task they required supernatural power, and they did not have it. Nothing is more pathetic than to see a child of God chopping away with a handle from which the axe head has fallen.

## PROMISE OF POWER

Ever since the Pentecostal outpouring, powerlessness in a Christian is absolutely without excuse, for the risen Lord promised power to His disciples. His very last words before His ascension carried this assurance: "Ye shall receive power, after that the Holy Ghost is come upon you: and ye shall be witnesses unto me both in Jerusalem, and in all Judea, and in Samaria, and unto the uttermost part of the earth" (Ac 1:8).

Christ claimed that the Father had invested Him with all power, celestial and terrestrial. "All power is given unto me in heaven and in earth." The Holy Spirit, gift of both Father and Son, personally communicates this power to the believer who recognizes the lordship of Christ and walks in fellowship with Him. To use the Old Testament figure, the anointing of the Head is available for all the members: "It is like the precious oil upon the head, that ran down upon the beard, even Aaron's beard: that went down to the skirts of his garments" (Ps 133:2).

The holy anointing oil with which the high priest was consecrated was so lavishly poured upon his mitered head that it streamed down upon his body, reaching even to the fringe of his priestly garments. Pentecost provides the interpretation of this beautiful symbolic act. On Christ, our Head and great High Priest, the Holy Spirit was poured out in unmeasured fullness, for "God giveth not the Spirit by measure unto him" (Jn 3:34). The Spirit was given in such profusion that the anointing reached His mystical body, even to its least member—to the very skirts of His garments.

The promised power becomes the believer's only by virtue of his union with Christ. It can neither be earned nor self-generated. The machinery in a factory works not by self-generated force, but by power derived through constant union with the dynamo. Break the union and the power ceases. Even so, as we abide in Christ we may momentarily be recipients of His power through the agency of His Spirit. "I am full of power by the spirit of the LORD," said Micah (3:8).

In an agricultural college a group of students decided to test the lifting power of a pumpkin. They constructed for it a harness of iron so keenly balanced that it would register on a scale exactly the power of the tiny pumpkin as it grew. As the days passed their astonishment increased. At first it lifted twenty pounds, then fifty pounds, then one hundred pounds. As the plant continued to grow, the scale registered five hundred pounds, then one thousand. Still its lifting power expanded the harness until it reached five thousand pounds. Surely this is the limit, they said. But it continued. And then they cut it from the vine. In an instant the power was gone. The scale dropped to zero. Separated from the vine it was powerless.

If we are true believers in Christ, we *are* united to Christ. Then why are so many believers spiritually powerless? Think of the man with the withered arm. The arm was united to his body, but it was nevertheless utterly powerless. Something had happened to the connecting nerves which prevented the life force from energizing the arm. May this not be the key to the absence of power in our lives? It is very possible that there may be some obstruction in the life which is hindering the communication of power. Before it will flow, the obstruction must be removed.

### NATURE OF POWER

Since power operates on many planes, we must discover its true nature.

#### NOT MERE MENTAL POWER

It is true that this spiritual power will greatly stimulate the intellect, but men of limited mental capacity

have enjoyed it in unusual degree. Dr. A. J. Gordon
wrote of Uncle John Vassar, a colporteur:

> He gave one literally a powerful electric shock the
> moment he touched him. There was such an intensity
> of zeal, accompanied with such a magnetic manner,
> that the impression was instantaneous and quite over-
> whelming. It was the lightning-like penetration of a
> piety that was always charged to the highest pitch. . . .
> Drowsy Christians started up when he came, as sleep-
> ing soldiers at bugle call.

Intellect can influence intellect, but the power of which
Jesus spoke had a wider reach than that.

### NOT MERE POWER OF PERSONALITY

Gifts of personality are enhanced by the incoming of
this power, but many an infidel possesses a most powerful personality. Such qualities are not confined to the
realm of the Holy Spirit.

### NOT RHETORICAL POWER ALONE

Many can sway an audience with their oratory, who
know nothing of spiritual power. If the sphere to
which one is called involves public ministry, the enduement of power will certainly result in increased effectiveness in utterance, but that is not in itself the power here
envisaged.

### NOT A POWER UNDER OUR CONTROL

God does not give us a something—power—which
we can control and use as we will. Simon coveted the
power which he saw Peter exercise, and asked, "Give
me also this power. . . . But Peter said to him, Your
silver perish with you, because you thought you could
obtain the gift of God with money."

A POWER SOVEREIGNLY BESTOWED BY GOD

It is not the awakening into new exercise of something that has been lying dormant within. Jesus said the power was "the Holy Spirit coming upon you." It is a Person whose presence brings power—the power, not of our personality but of the Holy Spirit's personality. To use a familiar figure, Christ is the power station, the Spirit the reticulating system. We are indwelt by Him and He communicates Christ's power to us so long as we abide in Him. In this lies the possibility of power-filled service.

Dr. F. B. Meyer once said, "I am only an ordinary man. I have no special gifts. I am no orator, no scholar, no profound thinker. If I have done anything for Christ and my generation, it is because I have given myself entirely to Jesus Christ and then tried to do whatever He wanted me to do." His long life of fruitful service demonstrated that spiritual power is experienced continuously where no obstacle is placed in the way of the working of the Holy Spirit.

## MANIFESTATION OF POWER

The conception of the enduement with power from on high, as Jesus termed it, is too often associated with the idea of ecstatic experience, as though that were an end in itself. But the emotional aspect of the experience is nowhere given prominence in the New Testament. That the enduement may be accompanied by exaltation of spirit no intelligent Christian would deny, but such an accompaniment is incidental, not essential. It is in large measure a matter of temperament.

Nor is this power necessarily conscious. On one occasion Rev. W. P. Nicholson, an evangelist who evidenced the power of the Spirit in unusual degree in his ministry, underwent special electric treatment in Edinburgh. He was asked to sit in a chair, and meanwhile the doctor read the newspaper. After waiting some time, he inquired when the treatment would begin.

"You are being treated now," replied the doctor.

"But I do not feel anything at all," responded the patient.

The doctor then took a board with several electric lamps on it and place it against his chest. Instantly they glowed with light.

"Mr. Nicholson," said the doctor, "there is enough electricity passing through your body to run a tramcar on the street. You do not feel it because you are insulated."

So we may have the power of Almighty God passing through us and yet be unconscious of the fact because there is no special call for its use. But whenever the need arises, the power will be manifested, for it is there.

The chief evidence of the possession of this power will be an unusual effectiveness in reaching the hearts of others. Witness will be spiritually fruitful. "Ye shall receive power . . . ye shall be witnesses unto me," was the Lord's promise. Nathanlike, we will be able to make those to whom we witness feel, "Thou art the man." Our testimony will reach the conscience, will make spiritual truths real, and will lead men to Christ.

There is an indefinable yet unmistakable difference between the empowered preacher and any other. Henry Moorhouse, converted pickpocket, stood up before a vast congregation in Belfast and did nothing else but repeat again and again John 3:16, when the most surprising results accrued. Souls were smitten with conviction of sin and gloriously converted. Without a word falling from his lips, the very presence of Charles G. Finney in a mill caused the operatives to weep tears of

contrition and, at a meeting held there, to yield in
scores to the claims of Christ.

But not all are called to preach. To some the enduement of power will be manifested in the ability to glorify
God in their appointed sphere, however humble, and to
discharge effectively the task assigned by the Head of
the church.

### EXAMPLES OF POWER

It is a fact of more than passing significance that the
Son of God would not venture on His public ministry
until endued with the Holy Spirit and power. In His
baptism at Jordan when the Spirit descended on Him as
a dove, He was, as in every spiritual experience, "the
firstborn among many brethren." It is surely clear that
if such an anointing was essential for His service, He
who had been filled with the Spirit from His birth, then
we fallen men need it a hundredfold more. And yet
most seem content to do without that which Christ
found indispensable.

In the years of our Lord's obscurity, although He fulfilled in every detail the will of God, He made no great
impression even in Nazareth. John the Baptist was shak-
ing the nation to its very foundations, from the king on
the throne to the peasant in the field, but Jesus made no
such stir until after the descent of the Spirit. Then all
was changed; God's clock had struck. Immediately His
missionary career began. He had read the Scripture lesson in the synagogue on many occasions previously, but
now the people are aware of a new note of authority as
He ministers. Every eye was glued on Him and "all
bare him witness, and wondered at the gracious words
which proceeded out of his mouth. And they said, Is
not this Joseph's son?" The difference was accounted

for in the very passage of Scripture which He read:
"The Spirit of the Lord is upon me, because he hath
anointed me to preach the gospel to the poor; he hath
sent me to heal the brokenhearted, to preach deliverance
to the captives . . . to set at liberty them that are bruised
(Lk 4:18).

These words referred to the Messiah, and we may be
tempted to ask whether there is any real parallel between His case and ours. Perhaps not in an absolute
sense, but what of the apostles? In obedience to their
Lord's command they tarried in Jerusalem until they
were endued with power from on high (Lk 24:49).
They suspended direct activity and testimony for the
time being, as they had been commanded. It is not difficult to imagine the heart-searching among them during
those memorable ten days as they recalled their past
failure and faced up to the vast implications of the
Great Commission. What puny resources for such a
staggering task! What complete absence of influence
and lack of qualifications! What helplessness, self-
despair, self-emptying!

Then came the heavenly gift, the divine anointing,
and the servants were as their Lord. See the transformation. The mighty Pentecostal preacher was none other
than the Peter who a few days before had three times
denied his Lord. The flaming love of the ambitious
James led him to prison and to death—the first martyr.
The fire-eating John was transformed into the apostle
of love. The timid became brave; the unstable, inflexi-
ble; the self-assertive, meek; and the carnal, spiritual.
Something had happened and they now began to turn
the world upside down.

There was undoubtedly a dispensational aspect of the
happenings on the day of Pentecost, but there was an

experimental side as well. The apostles must tarry in Jerusalem before they could be endued with power, but must we? So far as God is concerned, no. The Spirit has been given and the gift is for every believer. So far as we are concerned, the answer may be, yes—until we remove the hindrances which bar the path to power.

Speaking to a concourse of preachers at Mt. Hermon, Dwight L. Moody once said,

> There is no need to stop your work in order to wait for this enduement of power, but do not be satisfied until you get it. Young men, you will get this blessing when you seek it above all else. There will be no trouble about knowing when you have the power. We would not have to wait long for the enduement if we did not have to come to an end of ourselves. This sometimes is a long road. If God were to endue us with power when we are filled with conceit, we would become as vain as peacocks, and there would be no living with us.

## CONDITIONS OF POWER

A survey of relevant scriptures makes it abundantly clear that spiritual power is imparted only when the heart is in such a state of preparedness that it becomes right for God to communicate it to us in increasing measure by His Spirit.

He imparts His power on certain conditions.

### RENUNCIATION OF REVEALED SIN

The Psalmist voices the divine dictum, "If I regard [hold on to] iniquity in my heart, the Lord will not hear me" (Ps 66:18). We must honestly satisfy ourselves that we are harboring no known sin, and that there is not in our hearts a secret sympathy with sin. We should ask ourselves whether some wrong has been done to another which has never been confessed to them, some injury suffered at the hands of another which has never been forgiven, some sin for which no restitution has been made. Or it may be some wrongful indulgence of appetite or passion, some doubtful practice or conformity to the world. The Spirit who reveals the sin will enable the forsaking of it.

## WILLINGNESS TO DO GOD'S WILL

The person who desires to qualify for the reception of spiritual power no longer demands the right to have his own way. He will no longer hold back anything from God, nor will he hold back from anything God asks of him. The power is given solely for the purpose of enabling him to do God's will, not his own.

## A PASSION FOR CHRIST'S GLORY

God will delight to bestow the enduement when we are "willing to be rendered invisible by the investiture." When ye yearn not for spiritual pleasure or prominence, but supremely for His glory, the enduement with power is not far away. But if we seek it from selfish motives, our search is self-defeating.

## PRAYER AND APPROPRIATION

It was "as Jesus prayed" that He was anointed. It was as the disciples prayed that the Spirit descended. "It is the believer's privilege and duty to CLAIM a distinct anointing of the Spirit to qualify him for his work," wrote Dr. A. J. Gordon. We may meet every other condition and fail just here, for nothing can take the place of the appropriation of faith.

I take the promised Holy Ghost,
I take the power of Pentecost
To fill me to the uttermost,
    I take, He undertakes.

Now, if God is the owner of all, it is His right to appoint His own rental; and with a generosity beyond that which is accustomed to characterize the conduct of men, He has asked of earth's occupants but a small proportion of the increase of the land, namely, one-tenth. The apostles and prophets never disputed this nor yet did they neglect it; whether rich or poor, they regarded God's request and paid their tithe. As early as Cyprian's day in the third century, he excoriated those Christians who forgot their obligation, "Some of us do not even give tithes of our patrimony, and when God commands us to sell, we purchase and amass." Chrysostom, the golden-mouthed, cried, "Oh what a shame! that what was no great matter among the Jews should be pretended to be such among Christians. If there was danger then in omitting tithes, think how great must be the danger now!" Ambrose in the fourth century said, "The Lord commands our tithes to be paid every year. He has given you nine parts but He has reserved the tenth for Himself; and if you give not the tenth part to Him, He will take from you the nine parts. Whosoever is not willing to give those tithes to God which he has kept back, fears not God and knows not what true repentance and confession means." John Calvin declared that the heathen contributed more to their idols to express their superstitions than Christian people are giving to the great cause of Christ. Knox reminds us that our Lord in the Gospels, speaking to the Pharisees of the payment of tithes, said, "These ye ought to have done." It is only another instance of the great Apostle's teaching that "Whatsoever was written aforetime was written for our learning," and another confirmation of the fact that the Old and New Testaments are not opposing books but counterparts of one great volume, and that the mandate of the one is the moral law of the other.

W. B. RILEY

## 5

# THE LESSON OF STEWARDSHIP

> For ye know the grace of our Lord Jesus Christ,
> that, though he was rich, yet for your sakes he became
> poor, that ye through his poverty might be rich. There-
> fore . . . see that ye abound in this grace also (2 Co
> 8:9, 7).

THE INVESTOR who secured an investment free of income tax, estate, and inheritance tax would consider
himself fortunate indeed. And still more so if it were
unaffected by business depressions, devastating wars,
and calamities. Our Lord indicated that it was possible
to find such an investment. Speaking as financial Ad-
viser, He counseled:

> Lay not up for yourselves treasures upon earth,
> where moth and rust doth corrupt, and where thieves
> break through and steal: but lay up for yourselves
> treasures in heaven, where neither moth nor rust doth
> corrupt, and where thieves do not break through nor
> steal (Mt 6:19-20).

If it be asked how treasure in heaven may be amassed,
the answer is not hard to find. Of the seven days of each
week, God asks that one be reserved for Himself. Of the
income or salary with which He blesses us—and it is He
who gives us the power to earn wealth—He invites us
to reserve a proportion for the furtherance of His inter-

ests. This is not an unreasonable request, and yet in
practice His claim is ignored by the great majority of
Christians. Only a small minority regularly and sys-
tematically set aside a worthy sum for God's service.
Tithing is the method usually adopted, and a good beginning it is, but only a beginning.

There are those who object to tithing on the grounds
that it is a legalistic practice, and we are now no longer
under law but under grace. Such objectors forget that
tithing was practiced, obviously with God's sanction and
approval, four centuries before the law was given. "And
Melchizedek king of Salem . . . blessed him, and said,
Blessed be Abram of the most high God . . . And he
gave him tithes of all" (Gen 14:18-20).

## HINDRANCES TO LIBERALITY

The spread of the kingdom of God on earth and the
fulfillment of the risen Christ's missionary commission
depend in large measure on the money available for the
purpose. It is therefore not surprising that the adversary
employs many stratagems to dry up the fountains of
Christian liberality, thus preventing the release of funds
for world evangelization. His wiles are many.

He suggests *a postponement of generosity* until some
more convenient season. "I will give liberally to God,"
says the generous-hearted man, "when I am in a better
position financially to do so." The desire is worthy and
sincere, but observation proves that it is unlikely in the
extreme that this man will ever become a liberal giver,
unless he changes his attitude and gives now. It is gen-
erally fatal to stifle or postpone a generous impulse.

Robert G. LeTourneau, pioneer of earth-moving
equipment who gave 90 percent of his income to God's
work, as a younger man purposed to give liberally to

God in the following year when his financial position would be easier. In a year's time, instead of this being the case, he was facing bankruptcy. Only then did he learn the folly of postponing generosity. He immediately put things right on this point, and prosperity returned.

Another device adopted by the enemy is *to freeze the assets* of the willing-hearted steward so that he will have no liquid funds available for Christian enterprises. Either expanding business demands the reinvestment of every penny as soon as it is released, or existing investments require the sinking of more money to secure them. As a consequence, this man, though having all the goodwill in the world, is chronically impecunious when it comes to giving substantially to the Lord's work.

Yet another wile of the tempter is to neutralize any increase in income by encouraging *a proportionate increase in the standard of living*, so that no more is available than before the increase, but perhaps less. A new car, a larger home soon drain off any surplus.

How different was it with the selfless John Wesley, who from the sale of his books alone gave away between thirty and forty thousand pounds. In 1787 he told Samuel Bradburn, one of his preachers, that he never gave away less than one thousand pounds a year, and yet when he died, his personal estate amounted to only a few pounds. What was the secret of his sustained generosity?

It began in his early Christian life. When earning thirty pounds a year, he lived on twenty-eight pounds and gave the remaining two to the Lord's work. When the next year his salary was doubled he did not double his giving but increased it sixteen times over. "I lived comfortably on twenty-eight pounds last year," he said, "I can do so again." Instead of raising his standard of living he raised his standard of giving and presented the whole increase to his Lord. It is small wonder that God later entrusted him with so much of the true spiritual riches.

Some time ago a contributor to a missionary fund sent a check for twenty-five pounds. In the covering letter he stated that his family desired a new radio, but he was unwilling to spend so much on a luxury when there was such urgent need on the missionfield. Finally he resolved the problem by deciding that for every luxury bought for themselves, he would devote an equivalent amount to Christian work—an example worthy of emulation.

It cannot be too strongly stated that in the New Testament *there are no two standards of living taught*— one for the Christian worker or missionary whose support comes from the Lord's treasury and another for the businessman or worker at home. The missionary is equally entitled to the luxuries we enjoy at home if it comes to the matter of rights. If we have a car in the interests of our work, why should not the missionary have a car for his work? Since all we have is a gift and trust from our sovereign Lord, why should there be a double standard? Among followers of a cross-bearing Christ, the sacrifices in the interests of the gospel should be equal. In time of war it is recognized that equality of sacrifice is only fair. Is this principle less applicable in the truceless spiritual warfare in which we are engaged?

One final method adopted by Satan was styled by the late Dr. A. J. Gordon "extra-corpus benevolence." The deceiver persuades his victim *to postpone his generosity until after death*, by bequeathing a substantial sum to Christian organizations. In his trenchant manner Dr. Gordon emphasized the fact that a reward was promised in Scriptures only for *deeds done in the body*. The Christian is, of course, justified in making adequate provision for his dependents, but can it be truly called giving to God when, having made provision for his responsibilities, he holds onto the surplus until death shakes it from his pockets?

Great blessing has come to many who have put their money to work for the Lord during their lifetime. This is a true laying up of treasure in heaven. After speaking on this theme on one occasion the author was summoned by a businessman who said that he was that day disbursing £9,000 which he had left to various missionary societies in his will. He thus had the joy of seeing the fruitage of his gift in his lifetime.

## EXTENT OF LIBERALITY

It is relevant to inquire what the Scripture teaches concerning the proportion of our income which should be given to God. Jacob the swindler gave one-tenth. Zaccheus the despised taxgatherer gave one-half. The unnamed and impecunious widow gave "all her living." In the final analysis this question must be answered by the individual. But could it, in the light of Calvary, be less than one-tenth? Those who lived under the old covenant did not begin to give until the obligatory tenth had been paid. That was a first charge which could not be evaded. The zealous Jew gave at least one-sixth of his income to God. As a devout Jew, this would be our Lord's practice. And shall we who are enjoying all the benefits of His cross be content to give less than those who lived in the dim twilight of Mt. Sinai? "Freely ye have received, freely give."

In his book, *Your God and Your Gold*, L. B. Flynn writes:

To think that payment of our tithe discharges our financial obligation to God is a gross deception. Man's responsibility in regard to money involves far more than ten per cent. It encompasses the whole of his money. It is as though we have been given an expense account by the Lord. We must be able to justify the items we charge against it. Just as a travelling salesman would find it impossible to purchase from his expense account a fur coat for his wife and a bicycle for his boy, so many Christians should find it difficult to spend money with a clear conscience for extravagant and unnecessary luxuries.

In all true giving there is the element of sacrifice. The widow who gave her all was the classic example. The value of her gift was estimated not by its amount, but by the sacrifice it entailed. One man's gift of a tenth may involve far greater self-denial than another man's gift of nine-tenths. Our gifts will be appraised rather by what is left than by what is given.

Following an address on this theme, a letter was received from a Christian lady in an excellent position, from which this excerpt is taken:

> I have always tithed my income and I have thought I gave liberally to God's work. But I realize how little I have given, because I have quite a lot left, seeing I earn a good salary. The Lord has asked me to give Him half my income, and I do it joyfully, knowing that He will bless me with spiritual blessings.
>
> If in my love I have promised too much, I pray that He may help me to live on the other half, and will you pray that, if He wills me to give more, I shall claim the grace to do it for Him who has done so much for me.

At a convention, a young surgeon who had received

one thousand pounds compensation for the loss of the use of a finger through an accident, heard the call of God to sacrificial giving, and gave the whole amount in the missionary offering. At the same gathering an old lady, obviously with small means, handed in her gold watch, probably her only treasure, saying, "If there is an offering of jewellery I would like to give this watch."

It might be a disturbing question to some to be asked if they were in arrears with the Lord's portion. One businessman, convicted of his sin in withholding from God His rightful portion, called in an accountant and instructed him to make up a statement of his arrears. He then began to reduce his debt to God as he was able. Could it be that there is in the bank account of the reader money which by rights should be spreading the gospel in Africa or in Asia?

"Will a man rob God?" asked the prophet Malachi. Yes, he will if he gets the opportunity, for God rejoined, *"Yet ye have robbed Me. . . . In tithes and offerings"* (3:8).

## PROBLEMS OF LIBERALITY

Certain practical problems present themselves in the exercise of our stewardship.

A farmer faced a very real perplexity when he purposed in his heart to give God His portion in the future. Through an adverse season his payments were in arrears. Should he first overtake his arrears and then commence to give to God, or should he begin tithing at once? We suggested that this was a matter between himself and God, but asked this question, "When the state levies its social security tax, does it levy it on the income remaining after you have overtaken arrears, or does it regard the tax as a first charge?"

"It is certainly a first charge on my income," was the reply.

"Then your problem is to decide whether God, the state or your creditors should have priority. If you feel you should put your creditors first, no one could say you were wrong. But if you have faith to honor God by according Him first preference, He will doubtless enable you to meet all your obligations."

And the sequel? Although it was with a trembling faith, he began to tithe at once. During the ensuing year, a difficult one because of drought conditions, all his neighbors lost money, but he was able, not only to meet all outstanding accounts, but to reduce his indebtedness.

Irregularity of income in some occupations poses another problem, but where the will to honor God is present, a solution will be found. If the income is irregular, it can be tithed irregularly as soon as it is known. If there is a doubt, he who gives God the benefit of the doubt will be no loser.

## GIVING BY FAITH

On one occasion during a time of financial depression, the people at a convention were challenged at a missionary meeting to allow the element of faith to enter into their giving. After seeking God's face, they were asked to promise in faith what they believed He would have them give, even though they could not see at the moment how it could be done. If missionaries lived by faith, could they not give by faith? Six months later, the treasurer of the missionary fund received a check for twenty pounds from a young man. Again, six months later, a similar check arrived with the following letter:

When the appeal was made, challenging us to give by faith, I was unemployed, had no prospect of work and had nothing I could give. But I went aside with the Lord and was honest with Him. I said, "Lord, if Thou wilt entrust me with forty pounds during the coming year, I will give it to Thy work." Immediately I went home I got a job, I have not lost a day's work since then and honestly I am in a position I never dreamed I would be in a year ago.

Experience teaches that *the man who objects to tithing is the man who does not tithe,* and not unlikely his antipathy arises from the prickings of conscience. Where is the liberal giver to God who counts it a burden? When the Lord's portion is set aside with jealous and loving care, giving becomes a delight. The sum so consecrated is never missed, for it is never regarded as one's own.

A young father suddenly died as the result of a fatal disease. His total assets were his week's wages and the furniture in his home. He left a wife and three small children. During a trade depression his wages had been reduced to little more than four pounds a week. Throughout the fifteen years of their married life these two stewards, often at great personal sacrifice, had with meticulous care set aside ten shillings a week as the Lord's portion. Frequently it involved foregoing what to many would seem necessities, but whatever else was reduced, the Lord's tithe was kept sacrosanct.

Immediately after his death, money began to flow in to his widow from unexpected sources. On making up her accounts some time later, she found that the amount received was the exact equivalent of the amount they had devoted to the Lord during their married life, *but with interest added.* During those years while they had the joy of seeing their money at work for God in various parts of the world, they little dreamed that their heavenly Father had been carefully depositing it in His unfailing bank, only to return it with interest in their hour of need. She had no reason to regret being liberal in her giving to God.

Many years ago a lad of sixteen left home to seek his fortune. All his worldly possessions were tied up in a bundle. As he trudged along he met an old neighbor, the captain of a canal boat. A conversation which changed the whole current of the boy's life ensued.

"Well, William, where are you going?"

"I don't know," he answered. "Father is too poor to keep me at home any longer, and says I must now make a living for myself."

"There's no trouble about that," said the captain. "Be sure you start right and you'll get along fine."

William told his friend that the only trade he knew about was soap-making, at which he had helped his father while at home.

"Well," said the old man, "let me pray with you once more and give you a little advice, and I will let you go."

They knelt down on the towpath; the old man prayed earnestly for William and then offered this advice:

"Someone will soon be the leading soap-maker in New York. It can be you as well as anyone. I hope it may. Be a good man; give the Lord all that belongs to Him of every dollar you earn; make an honest soap; give a full pound, and I am certain you will yet be a rich and prosperous man."

When the boy arrived in the city, he found it hard to get work. Lonesome and far from home, he remembered the last words of the canal-boat captain. He was led to "seek first the kingdom of God and his righteousness," and united with the church.

On securing work, he remembered his promise to the captain, and the first dollar he earned brought up the question of the Lord's part. Reading in his Bible that the Jews were commanded to give one-tenth, he said, "If the Lord will take one tenth, I will give that." After that, ten cents of every dollar was sacred to the Lord.

He soon became a partner in the business in which he worked. After a few years, his partner died and William became the sole owner. He resolved to keep his word to the old captain. He made an honest soap, gave a full pound, and instructed his bookkeeper to open an account with the Lord, carrying one-tenth of his income to that account.

He prospered. His business grew. His family was blessed. His soap sold, and he grew rich faster than he had ever hoped. He gave the Lord two-tenths and prospered more than ever. Then he gave three-tenths; then four-tenths, then five-tenths. He educated his family, settled his plans for life, and thereafter gave all his income to the Lord.

Who was the lad? William Colgate. And who has not heard of Colgate's soaps?

When we stand before the judgment throne to give an account of our stewardship, how will we wish we had administered the money entrusted to us by our Master?

> What I spend, I lose;
> What I keep will be left to others;
> What I give away will remain for ever mine.

We have noted a difference between the *guilt* and the *pollution* of sin. This is of importance for a clear understanding of the matter; but in actual life we must ever remember that they are not thus divided. God through the blood deals with sin as a whole. Every true operation of the blood manifests its power simultaneously over the *guilt* and the *pollution* of sin. Reconciliation and cleansing always go together, and the blood is ceaselessly operative.

Many seem to think that the blood is there, so that if we have sinned again, we can turn again to it to be cleansed. But this is not so. Just as a fountain flows always and always purifies what is placed in it or under its stream, so it is with this Fountain, opened for sin and uncleanness (Zech 13:1). The eternal power of life of the Eternal Spirit works through the blood. Through Him the heart can abide always under the flow and cleansing of the blood.

In the Old Testament cleansing was necessary for each sin. In the New Testament cleansing depends on Him who ever lives to intercede. When faith sees and desires and lays hold of this fact, the heart can abide every moment under the protecting and cleansing of the blood.

ANDREW MURRAY

# 6

# THE LESSON OF CLEANSING

For if the blood of bulls and of goats, and the ashes of an heifer sprinkling the unclean, sanctifieth to the purifying of the flesh: how much more shall the blood of Christ, who through the eternal Spirit offered himself without spot to God, purge your conscience from dead works to serve the living God? (Heb 9:13-14).

NOTHING IS MORE TYRANNICAL and intolerable than a defiled conscience, a conscience polluted by sin and oppressed with guilt. Once aroused, it refuses to be silenced. Even in the holiest moments it insinuates its message of condemnation. Communion with God is effectively cut off. Boldness of access into His presence becomes only a wistful memory. The light of His countenance is shadowed and the subtle enemy is able to gain an easy victory. Joy takes wings and service becomes a weary drudgery. The possibility of heart peace and victory seems an ever receding mirage. And all this because the conscience has been defiled.

It is surely not possible that God has made provision for every other longing and need of the human heart, and not for the cleansing of the polluted conscience. There must be some panacea for this distressing malady of the soul. And there is.

The reference to the ashes of a heifer in Hebrews

9:13-14 carries us back to the picture gallery of the Old Testament and especially to the strange ceremony recorded in Numbers 19. It is surprising to find this ordinance of the red heifer, not in Leviticus, the priest's manual, as we would expect, but in Numbers, the book of Israel's pilgrimage. It is striking that in each book of the Pentateuch there is one outstanding chapter which foreshadows some distinctive aspect of the death of Christ.

In Genesis 22, which records the offering of Isaac by Abraham, the reader is brought face to face with the inwardness of the mysterious transaction of the cross. The infinite cost to the Father of the sacrifice of the Son is there pictured, as is the willingness of the Son to perform His Father's will in the divine plan of redemption.

The record of the Passover night in Exodus 12 represents the blood of the innocent victim applied in faith as availing to stay the execution of judgment. Because of the blood, the Avenger becomes the Protector.

Another double picture is presented in Leviticus 16 which details the ritual of the great Day of Atonement. The death of Christ is there represented as both satisfying the righteous claims of God against the sinning man, and forever bearing away his polluting sins "into a land not inhabited."

In Numbers 19, read in conjunction with Hebrews 9:13-14, we are introduced to the death of Christ as making a standing provision for the constant cleansing of the Christian as he walks amid the inescapable defilements of his daily life. It is God's provision for the maintenance of unbroken communion with Him. Sins of the future are in view as well as sins of the past, and sins of which we are unconscious as well as those of which we are conscious.

It must be noted that the provisions of this chapter put no premium on sin. It harmonizes entirely with Paul's question and answer, "Shall we continue in sin? God forbid" (Ro 6:1-2). The objective John had in view for the believers was clearly expressed: "My little children, these things write I unto you, that ye sin not" (1 John 2:1). But in the same passage he recognizes the possibility of sinning and reveals the remedy for such a condition. The sinning is no longer necessary, but it is possible and therefore must be provided for. The lifeboat is provided, not because the vessel *must* sink, but in case it does. The ordinance under consideration was such a divine provision. It is one of the richest in spiritual teaching of the Old Testament types and will amply repay close study, for Paul assures us that "all these things happened unto them for ensamples [types, margin]: and they are written for our admonition, upon whom the ends of the world are come" (1 Co 10:11).

## POLLUTION BY SIN

Of all diseases, sin is the most contagious. It inevitably brings pollution in its train. In Numbers 19 this fact is emphasized by the constant repetition of the word *unclean* which occurs no fewer than fifteen times. We are polluted by the sin that is within as well as by the sin that is without.

### CAUSES OF POLLUTION

These are clearly defined, and in every case are concerned with contact with death in one way or another. As sin is the cause and occasion of death, so death is the outward and visible sign of the presence of sin. Sin is spiritual death. At the time the ordinance of the red heifer was given, death was taking a terrible toll of the doomed generation of Israelites who had in unbelief refused to enter the promised land. As many as one hundred would be dying every day, and hundreds would be rendered unclean through their participation in the funeral rites. But God graciously did not leave the stricken people without an avenue of relief.

.Pollution could come to an Israelite *through touching a dead body* (v. 2), typifying actual contact with sin, acts of sin for which he was personally responsible. With many there is definite, conscious sin which must be confessed and dealt with before harmony can replace the discord of the soul. Or it could come *through entering a tent where a dead body lay* (v. 14). Even though actual contact had not taken place, the effect was the same. Companionship and intercourse with evil issues in pollution. Our sinless Lord could eat with publicans and sinners without sullying His own holiness, but this dirty world leaves its defiling marks on our robes. We cannot escape defilement. The conversation, books, newspapers, jokes and advertisements of the world all bring their own quota of pollution.

The very atmosphere is represented as being charged with pollution, for *every vessel left uncovered in the presence of death* (v. 15) was unclean. The undetected contagion of sin can be active even in the home. For example, while radio and television have great cultural and spiritual value, if programs are not carefully selected they can be the unconscious means of allowing the atmosphere of the world to subtly infiltrate the sanctuary of the home. In the presence of evil, all our faculties require to be guarded—a watch set on the lips, the eye averted from the defiling sight, the ear closed to the impure word. Only thus can we escape the pollution of sin.

Even so insignificant a thing as *the accidental touching of a bone* (v. 16) brought consequences as severe as the touching of a dead body. The contamination of small sins is as great as that of what we mistakenly call big sins. All sins are the same size. They cannot be divided into great or small. Sin is so vile and contaminating in God's sight that the very slightest contact with it defiles the whole man. A thought, an imagination, a glance can as effectively obscure God's face as an open act of sin.

Even *in the open fields* (v. 16) the Israelite was not immune to defilement. Go where he will—into the secluded monastery or into the busy market—the Christian is never beyond the contaminating power of sin. It is inescapable. Thomas à Kempis recognized that "there is no order so holy, no place so secret, where there will be no temptation."

The man who *unconsciously walked over a grass-covered grave* (v. 16) totally oblivious of the corpse beneath his feet, did not escape pollution. Concealed sin, of whose presence we with our dulled spiritual perception are unconscious, can cloud our intercourse with the holy God who hates sin. We sin sufficiently even according to our own imperfect standards. But how much more must our holy God detect. Therefore, to be adequate, whatever provision God makes must provide for unconscious transgression as well as positive sin. Our self-knowledge is very imperfect, for we are always biased in our own favor. "I know nothing against myself," said Paul, "yet am I not hereby justified" (1 Co 4:4, ASV). He recognized that within him was a world of unrealized sin.

In this typical ordinance, God very vividly expresses His abhorrence of sin of every degree and indicates the sensitiveness of the Holy Spirit to sins both large and small, committed or inherent in our nature. This is strikingly illustrated in the communal life of the Maori race in New Zealand. The *tapu* (uncleanness), regarded among the Maoris as attaching to the man who has handled the dead, is such that, not only can he not enter any house or come into contact with any person without conveying defilement, but he may not even put forth his hands to the food he himself eats.

CONSEQUENCES OF POLLUTION

Under the old economy, pollution resulting from contact with death involved drastic consequences. Not only was the unclean person excluded from the camp, but, more seriously still, he was deprived of the service of the sanctuary. The results of sin, though outwardly different, are no less serious today. Sin in the Christian is much more culpable than sin in the man of the world, for guilt is always proportioned to privilege. It as surely interrupts fellowship with God as ceremonial uncleanness debarred the ancient offender from entering the house of the Lord.

The writer of the epistle to the Hebrews asserts that the works of the person whose conscience is defiled, are only "dead works" and therefore totally unacceptable to God. Dead works can never satisfy the living God. They are just what the words imply—activities in which there is no breath of the life-giving Spirit; activities prompted by the busy self-life; works which may be right in themselves but spring from unspiritual motives. Prayers that are heartless, preaching that is powerless, service that is loveless—these are dead works. The underlying reason is that there is a defilement through sin which demands a cleansing so deep that only the blood of Christ can effect it.

If it were possible for us to live to ourselves and not to influence and affect other lives, the consequences might not be so serious. But the solemn closing words of the chapter preclude any such possibility: "And whatsoever the unclean person toucheth shall be unclean" (v. 22). When out of touch with God, we are harming others with every breath we draw. Instead of being a savour of life as God intends, we become a savour of death.

> Only a word, yes, only a word
> That the Spirit's small voice whispered, Speak!
> But the worker passed onward, unblest and weak
> Whom you were meant to have stirred
> To courage, devotion and love anew,
> Because when the message came to you,
>     You were OUT OF TOUCH with your Lord.
>
> Only a note, yes, only a note
> To a friend in a distant land,
> The Spirit said, Write, but then you had planned
> Some different work, and you thought
> It mattered little, you did not know
> 'Twould have saved a soul from sin and woe,
>     You were OUT OF TOUCH with your Lord.

## PURIFICATION FOR SIN

If our case is as bad as represented, then we require a radical remedy which probes as deep as the disease. Such a remedy is suggested by the ordinance.

### THE TYPICAL RITE

No part of the ceremony lacks significance. If we

assumed the role of inquiring spectators, we would observe some representative Israelites leading a red heifer to the high priest. Why red? Why not black, since it is to be a sin-offering? Perhaps because red and not black is the color used in the Bible for sin. "Though your sins be as scarlet . . . though they be red like crimson . . ." (Is 1:18). Or perhaps because it foreshadowed the mediatorial work of Christ which was "all pure crimson." It must be "a red heifer without spot, wherein is no blemish, and upon which never came yoke" (v. 2).

Great care had been taken in the selection of the victim. More than three hairs together of any color other than red were sufficient to lead to its disqualification. It had to be without spot externally. Nor could it have borne a yoke, for females were considered to have been marred if so used. Eleazer officiated in the place of his father Aaron, who would have been unclean and thus unfitted for his responsibility had he performed the ceremony. There were further instructions to be observed:

> Ye shall give her unto Eleazer the priest, that he may bring her forth without the camp, and one shall slay her before his face: and Eleazer . . . shall . . . sprinkle of her blood directly before the tabernacle of the congregation seven times (vv. 3-4).

The blood of the heifer had to be sprinkled before the tabernacle in which dwelt God whose holiness had been so grievously outraged, and who alone could cleanse from sin.

> And one shall burn the heifer . . . and the priest shall take cedar wood, and hyssop, and scarlet [wool], and cast it into the midst of the burning of the heifer. . . . And a man that is clean shall gather up the ashes

of the heifer, and lay them . . . in a clean place (vv. 5-9).

From 1 Kings 4:33 we learn that the cedar and the hyssop, the greatest and least of the trees, fittingly represent human nature at its best and its worst, the natural life from its strongest side to its weakest. Around these was bound scarlet wool (Heb 9:19). The whole was burnt to ashes (apparently in order to conserve the offering for application), and the ashes were collected and stored in a clean place to which the conscience-stricken Israelite could quickly resort. The method of application was as follows: A clean person mixed a little ash with runnning water, dipped a bunch of hyssop in this "water of separation," and on the third and seventh days sprinkled the offender who was then fit to enjoy the service of the sanctuary once more. Such was the ritual.

## THE ANTITYPICAL REALIZATION

From the nature of the case the antitype always excels the type, and in indicating the significance of the ordinance, the writer to the Hebrews makes this abundantly clear: "If . . . the ashes of an heifer sprinkling the unclean, sanctifieth to the purifying of the flesh: *How much more* shall the blood of Christ . . . purge your conscience" (Heb 9:13-14).

Like the chosen victim, Christ was without spot or blemish. Through the miracle of the virgin birth and the activity of the Holy Spirit, He escaped the taint of original sin. His purity was essential and inherent. The word *blemish* is derived from Momus, the god of criticism. No matter how severe the criticism to which He was subjected during His life on earth it was demon-

strated that " in him is no sin" (1 Jn 3:5). The yoke of
sin never rested on His shoulders, nor was it under a
yoke of constraint that He consented to become the sacrifice for our sins. His sacrifice was absolutely volun-
tary.

Then, too, like the victim, Christ, in order "that he
might sanctify the people with his own blood, suffered
without the gate" of Jerusalem (Heb 13:12), the place
frequented by the lepers and defiled. The defilement
was viewed as transferred to the victim which must now
take the place of the defiled person—without the camp.
In this act of matchless condescension on the part of
the Lord of glory, the boundless and forgiving love of
God is exhibited. The sprinkling of the blood before
the tabernacle did not in itself effect the cleansing of
the polluted person, but before there can be purification
there must first be atonement.

The burning of the cedar and hyssop bound with
scarlet wool signifies that the sinful self-life, the "old
man" whether in attractive or repulsive guise, was cast
into the burning or, to use the New Testament figure,
was crucified with Christ, and in Him was done away
(Ro 6:6, RV). The self-life will always defile and pol-
lute unless we keep it in the place of death (Ro 6:11).
We must resolutely disregard its plea to be allowed to
come down from the cross.

The ashes, evidence of a completed sacrifice, were
regarded as the concentration of the essential properties
of the offering. They were incorruptible, and therefore
a suitable emblem of the perfection and everlasting
efficacy of the sacrifice of Christ. The ashes laid up in
a clean place represent the store of merit there is in the
Lord Jesus, perpetually preserved for the removal of
the daily pollution of sin. The smallest quantity of the

concentrated ash would suffice to cleanse. Jewish tradition records that only six heifers were required in all Jewish history. "If . . . the ashes of an heifer . . . *how much more* shall the blood of Christ."

## Purging from Sin

The elaborate ritual of the ordinance was of value only if those who, conscious of their defilement, availed themselves of its cleansing efficacy. Of what value to the defiled conscience of the Christian is the blood of Christ if he does not avail himself of its purging power?

### ACCESSIBILITY OF THE REMEDY

The ashes were kept in store in a readily accessible and clean place outside the camp, so that the distressed Israelite might without delay avail himself of the divine provision for cleansing. He need make no long pilgrimage to obtain the longed-for peace of conscience. Here again the antitype far excels the type. Even after he had complied with the ritual, the defiled man remained cut off from fellowship with God for seven days. But since Calvary, no long estrangements are necessary. The blood of Christ is always accessible and available to purge the defiled conscience the very moment we in faith avail ourselves of its cleansing properties, and it is at once efficacious to bring us back into communion with God. Our restoration can be as immediate as that experienced by David: "And David said unto Nathan, I have sinned against the LORD. And Nathan said unto David, The LORD also hath put away thy sin" (2 Sa 12:13).

### APPLICATION OF THE REMEDY

Before application, the ashes must be mingled with

running water—always a symbol of the Holy Spirit who alone can apply to our hearts the benefits of the mediatorial work of Christ. It is He who in love makes us conscious of our pollution, and then reveals the value and virtue of the blood of Christ. The seven-times sprinkled blood assures us of the purification made in heaven by our great High Priest, but on earth it is the Holy Spirit who makes the sacrifice efficacious to cleanse the defiled conscience.

The hyssop with which the water of purification was applied represents faith, powerless in itself to bring any relief, and yet capable of linking us to the infinite power and provision of God. It is not sufficient to know of this wonderful provision for cleansing the conscience; it must be individually appropriated.

Do we need this purging of the conscience from dead works? Is the sky above us clear? Are our lives a sweet savor of Christ? Are our prayers being answered? Is our work producing spiritual fruit? Perhaps the reason for our failures is that our consciences are defiled and our works are largely dead works. Then let us avail ourselves of God's provision for the restoration of unbroken fellowship. With the blood of Christ perpetually accessible and eternally available, we need remain not one hour longer estranged from God. Let it not be said of us that, "the word preached did not profit them, not being mixed with faith in them that heard it" (Heb 4:2).

The practical lesson taught us by the fact that there was a first Covenant, that its one special work was to convince of sin, and that without it the New Covenant could not come, is just what many Christians need. At conversion they were convinced of sin by the Holy Spirit. But this had chiefly reference to the guilt of sin, and in some degree to its hatefulness. But a real knowledge of the power of sin, of their entire and utter impotence to cast it out or to work in themselves what is good, is what they did not learn at once. And until they have learned this, they cannot possibly enter fully into the blessing of the New Covenant. It is when a man sees that, as little as he could raise himself from the dead, can he make or keep his own soul alive, that he becomes capable of appreciating the New Testament promise, and is made willing to wait on God to do all in him.

Do you feel that you are not fully living in the New Covenant, that there is still somewhat of the Old Covenant spirit of bondage in you? Do come, and let the Old Covenant finish its work in you. Accept its teaching, that all your efforts are failures.

ANDREW MURRAY

# 7

# THE LESSON OF INDWELLING
## SIN

Behold, the days come, saith the LORD, that I will make a new covenant with the house of Israel, and with the house of Judah: not according to the covenant that I made with their fathers in the day that I took them by the hand to bring them out of the land of Egypt; which my covenant they brake (Jer 31:31-32).

TO THE GREAT LOSS of the church, the rich vein of truth contained in the scriptural teaching concerning the old and new covenants is practically unexplored and unexploited today. In order that we may mine some of the hidden treasures, it is necessary to ask, What is a covenant?

## DEFINITION OF A COVENANT

A covenant is a mutual agreement of solemn and binding force between two parties. All who engage in the daily business of life are familiar with contracts and covenants, but in Bible times the word carried a deeper significance. The Hebrew word *berith* signifies "coming to an agreement through a divided sacrifice." An illustration of this is found in Genesis 15:9-10. In ratify-

ing a covenant, it was customary to cut the sacrificial
victim in two parts. Half was placed on each side of
two altars, between which the contracting parties passed.
Jeremiah makes reference to the rite: "And I will give
the men that have transgressed my covenant, which have
not performed the words of the covenant which they had
made before me, when they cut the calf in twain, and
passed between the parts thereof" (34:18). The rite
added solemnity and irrevocability to the covenant.

This word *covenant* frequently occurs in the Bible
and formed the very marrow of Puritan theology. It
gave to those virile and valiant Scottish Christians the
name of Covenanters. It is unfortunate that the word
has gone out of theological fashion, for the very divi-
sions of our Bible owe their titles to the fact that the
one enshrines the records of God's dealings with His
people under the old covenant while the other unfolds
the blessings of the new. If it be asked why a covenant
is necessary, the answer is simple: because men cannot
trust each other. The very fact of a covenant being
necessary is an evidence of a lack of confidence between
the parties. We ask those to sign or enter a solemn
agreement whose word we do not fully trust. No written
covenant is needed between trusted friends.

Is it not an astounding thought that God, knowing
this custom of men who have every reason for not trust-
ing one another, should descend to their level, and consent to bind Himself by a covenant—as though He, too,
could not be trusted? What purpose could He have in
view in such an act of condescension? Simply that He
desired to regain man's lost confidence in Him and
restore to man that perfect trust which he lost at the
fall when he fled in fear from the presence of God.

### CHARACTERISTICS OF THE OLD COVENANT

The old covenant is described or defined in several passages.

> He declared unto you his covenant, which he commanded you to perform, even ten commandments (Deu 4:13).
> If ye hearken to these judgments, and keep, and do them, . . . the LORD thy God shall keep unto thee the covenant (Deu 7:12).

The old covenant is, then, the Mosaic law as given on Mt. Sinai. In enunciating the terms of the new covenant, Jeremiah contrasted it with the old and identified it with the law of Moses: "I will make a new covenant . . . not according to the covenant that I made with their fathers in the day that I took them by the hand to bring them out of the land of Egypt; which my covenant they brake" (31:31-32).

#### IMPERFECT

The writer of the Hebrews epistle says that this covenant was imperfect: "The law made nothing perfect" (7:19); "If that first covenant had been faultless, then should no place have been sought for the second" (8:7).

It was not that the law was not a perfect code of morals, but it was imperfect in that its blessings were conditional on human obedience, and man was unable to meet its lofty demands. Instead of making "the comer thereunto perfect," it sent him away in despair. But as Paul writes in his letter to the Galatians, it had its ministry as a school master, to bring us to Christ.

#### IMPOTENT

Then, too, it was impotent: "What the law could not do, in that it was weak through the flesh . . ." (Ro 8:3).

Paul does not contend that there is any inherent weakness in the law itself or he would be contradicting his statement in the previous chapter that "the law is holy and righteous and good." The fatal defect and weakness is not in the law itself but in the flesh. We are the cause of the failure, not the law. The old covenant tells us what we should do or refrain from doing, what we should be and not be; but like the priest and the Levite in the parable, it leaves us helpless and half dead by the roadside. The law, while perfect in itself, is powerless to reproduce in us the holiness it commands.

IMPOSSIBLE

Not only is the law impotent, but its absolute observance is impossible: "They that are in the flesh cannot please God" (Ro 8:8).

We need only survey Israel's typical history to find abundant corroboration of this statement, and our personal experience too often bears melancholy testimony to its verity. Have we not often tried our utmost to please God, resolved never again to yield to sin's blandishments, only to fail once more? It is not that we *will not* fulfill the law of God, but we *cannot*. Its demands are so exacting that it is impossible of human fulfillment.

It might reasonably be asked, if it is impossible of fulfillment, why did God ask something which He knew to be impossible? This question involves the whole purpose God had in view in giving the covenant of law. When he created man, He endowed him with the most Godlike of all His attributes, free will or self-determination. He created man perfect and in full fellowship with Himself, and yet master of his own destiny. But the fall disrupted relations with his Maker and fellowship was rudely broken. Confidence turned to craven fear. Ever since Eden, God has been working to rescue man from the results of his own sin, and to restore the old relationship of mutual trust and confidence. He could, of course, achieve this by one word of His power, but only at the cost of man losing his free will, and God always respects the sanctity of human personality.

While God knew man's inability to keep His laws, man was quite ignorant of the fact. This was the method God adopted of educating him to his own incurable impotence and sinfulness, in order that he might once again be wholly cast upon Him for all. In no other way could the human and divine wills each be given their own rightful place.

### INDISPENSABLE

Thus it is seen that this covenant was indispensable to man's spiritual development and to the furthering of his highest interests. Man must be given abundant opportunity of demonstrating to his own satisfaction what he can do, and the old covenant was admirably adapted to the purpose.

### PURPOSE OF THE COVENANT

This was, in brief, to teach man two great and indispensable lessons, the mastering of which was essential to full fellowship with God.

First, *sin* in its awfulness and tremendous power: "By the law is the knowledge of sin" (Ro 3:20); "The law entered, that the offence might abound" (Ro 5:20); "That sin by the commandment might become exceeding sinful" (Ro 7:13).

The deadliness of a disease is not gauged by the patient's sense of its gravity. Many a victim of a fatal disease is insensible to pain. It is rather by the drastic measures adopted by the surgeon to cure it that we learn its seriousness. So the gravity and seriousness of sin are seen only in the measures adopted by God at Calvary to arrest its death-dealing influence. The cross of Christ is the measuring stick of the sinfulness of sin. The old covenant was given to teach man his powerlessness to cope with it unaided, for man's best efforts to fulfill the terms of the covenant found their fruitage in the tragedy of Calvary. The resurrection ushered in the new covenant.

Second, *holiness*, its beauty and eminent desirability, and man's own helplessness to attain to it: "The law is holy, and the commandment holy, and just, and good" (Ro 7:12); "The beauty of holiness" (Ps 96:9).

The old covenant set up God's standard of holiness— so lofty that man by his own efforts could never reach it, for that standard is perfection. In the heart in which the old covenant has done its work, the conviction is born, "If ever I am to become holy, God must do it for I cannot." This attitude provides the Holy Spirit with the opportunity He desires to conform us to the image of Christ.

### THE OUTCOME OF THE OLD COVENANT

"They continued not in my covenant" (Heb 8:9); "Which my covenant they brake" (Jer 31:32). The old covenant was inaugurated with awe-inspiring accompaniments, calculated to impress the nation with the solemnity of the occasion. When God came down to Sinai the whole mountain was filled with smoke and quaked greatly. Out of the thick darkness which shrouded the mountain came the voice of a trumpet, waxing exceeding loud, which proclaimed the ten words of the covenant. Trembling with abject fear in the distance, the people pleaded with Moses that they might hear that voice no more.

But, in spite of the majestic manifestation of the presence of God, no permanent impression was made on them. When the terms of the covenant were announced, they glibly assented to them, saying, "All the words that the Lord hath spoken will we do." Yet, even while Moses was carrying the engraved tables of stone down the mountainside, Israel had already broken the first of the commandments. And God's first act under the dispensation of law was an act of grace, or the whole nation would have perished.

Man's subsequent efforts to discharge his responsibilities under the old covenant met with no more success. The consistent pattern has been one of unrelieved failure. God longed to fulfill His part of the covenant, but has been precluded from doing so because man has failed to keep his.

## The Lesson of the Old Covenant

"In me, that is, in my flesh, dwelleth no good thing: for to will is present with me, but to do that which is good is not. For the good which I would I do not: but the evil which I would not, that I practice" (Ro 7:18-19, ASV). The reason God permits His children to experience humiliating and bitter defeat is that the old covenant has not completed its work. They have not yet been brought to the point of self-despair. Hope of self-improvement has not yet died. They still endeavor to fulfill the terms of the covenant in their own strength. They have not yet mastered the lesson which has been set.

When Dr. C. I. Scofield was expounding chapters 7 and 8 of the epistle to the Romans, he was showing the transition from the defeat of chapter 7 into the victory of chapter 8.

"What was the matter with St. Paul?" asked a man in the class. "Why did he find it hard to be good? I don't find it very hard to be good."

"What do you mean by being good?" asked Dr. Scofield.

"Living a clean life, being honest, paying my debts, treating people right, putting my hand in my pocket and helping my neighbor when he needs it."

"Oh," replied Dr. Scofield, "St. Paul did those things all his life. Any gentleman would do those things. Paul was not talking of that when he spoke of the struggle to be good."

"Well, what *did* he mean?" he asked, somewhat taken aback.

"Did you ever try to be meek?"

"No, sir, I don't admire a meek man."

"Don't you? Well, God does. His Son was meek and lowly. Now tell me, would you find it easy to be meek whatever happened?"

"I couldn't, that is not in my line. I'm not built that way."

Nor are most of us built to be meek, patient, long-suffering, humble, uncritical and unselfish under all circumstances. We should, therefore, acknowledge our inability to attain to the divine standard of holiness, and accept without reserve the teaching of the old covenant that our best efforts will result only in the cry of Romans 7: "O wretched man that I am. Who shall deliver me from this body of death?"

Many believers, although living in the dispensation of

the new covenant, in practice are living under the old. Justified by faith, they are striving to be sanctified by works. Having begun in the Spirit, they endeavor to be made perfect in the flesh. They are partly carnal, partly spiritual and thus involved in an increasing inward civil war. They are "stuck between Easter and Pentecost."

God will not tolerate a mixed life. He is as jealous of order in the spiritual realm as in the realm of nature. An ox was not allowed to plow with an ass. The farmer was not permitted to sow mixed seeds. The priest's garments could not be woven partly of linen, partly of wool. Ishmael, son of the bondwoman, could not live under the same roof as Isaac, son of the free woman. "Cast out the bondwoman and her son" was the divine command.

This principle is crystal clear in the Scriptures, and yet we are so slow to conform to God's requirements. Our lives and motives are strangely mixed. We desire to have "some of self and some of Thee." Our very humility tends to feed our pride, our kindnesses to nourish our self-esteem. Everything we do is tainted from the polluted fountains of the heart.

## THE PREDICTION OF THE NEW COVENANT

Jeremiah utterly despaired of Israel prospering on the basis of the old covenant. With divine illumination he predicted a day when the bankrupt old covenant would be superseded by another, entirely new, which would remedy all the defects of the old. It would not only command but empower. It would not only demand but provide. It would be safeguarded and furnished with provisions ensuring against failure.

A disappointed and defeated believer might object that he doubts neither God's willingness nor ability to give him deliverance, but it is his own inherent weakness that he fears. It was to meet this very weakness that the new covenant was provided. Had we not been weak and unable to deliver ourselves, the old would have sufficed.

We can easily discover whether in experience we are living under the old covenant or the new. If we are still living under the old, our lives will be characterized more by sighs than by songs. We will more often be vanquished than victorious, enslaved than emancipated.

> Bound, who should be conquerors,
> Slaves, who should be free.

Life will know more of turmoil than tranquillity. We will give the impression of being paupers rather than princes. Our outlook will be one of hopelessness instead of happiness.

If this is a true diagnosis of our condition, we should once and for all accept the lesson of the old covenant, and turn to the alluring promises of the new which are set forth in chapter 8.

The formula of the Old Covenant is, "Thou shalt not." These great words, like a flash of lightning, discovered to man what lies in the depths of his own being—moral obligation along with a sense of utter impotence to meet it, darkness and despair as of chaos returning.

The formula of the New Covenant is "I will"; still greater words, which discover the heights above, as it were the body of heaven in its clearness, unruffled serenity and easy self-achievement of the grace of God. It would not be possible to represent what is characteristic in each dispensation more vividly than by these contrasted formulas. On the one side is a vain effort to attain, a strife between the law of the mind and the law of the members, a sense of hopeless duality that carries unrest—noble if you will but not less fatal—to the centre of a man's being. On the other side is the rest of faith, a great reserve of spiritual power, the reconciliation of divine ideals with the practice of human lives achieved by grace. Moral obligation persists under the gospel, but only as it is resolved into the higher freedom of the new life. As Pascal says, "The law demands what it cannot give; grace gives all it demands."

GREAT TEXTS OF THE BIBLE.

# 8

# THE LESSON OF LIBERTY

For this is the covenant that I will make with the house of Israel after those days, saith the Lord; I will put my laws in their mind, and write them in their hearts: and I will be to them a God, and they shall be to me a people: and they shall not teach every man his neighbour, and every man his brother, saying, Know the Lord: for all shall know me, from the least to the greatest. For I will be merciful to their unrighteousness, and their sins and their iniquities will I remember no more. In that he saith, A new covenant, he hath made the first old. Now that which decayeth and waxeth old is ready to vanish away (Heb 8:10-13).

THERE WAS NO DEFECT or flaw in the old covenant as God gave it, although Israel failed so grievously in keeping it. The root cause of trouble was that man's heart was not right with God, and rebelled strongly against His law. As Paul put it, "The carnal mind is enmity with God." If a remedy was to be found for man's chronic inability to meet the demands of divine holiness, it had to provide adequate motive power, and thus counteract the fatal bias of man's nature. All this God did in the new covenant. It will help us in our study of the subject to hold clearly in our minds the fundamental contrasts between the old and new covenants.

### CONTRASTS OF THE COVENANTS

The *old covenant* showed man what he ought to do, but bestowed on him neither the disposition nor the power to do it. It demanded what it could not give. The *new covenant*, on the contrary, gives all it demands. This glorious truth was appreciated by St. Augustine who expressed it in his prayer, "O, God, give what Thou commandest, then command what Thou wilt." When once the heart, the source, is put right, correct actions flow spontaneously.

The *old covenant* finally proved to man's satisfaction —and yet dismay—that he could not by himself keep God's law. It was a staggering and disillusioning revelation of the futility of his best efforts. The *new covenant* was given to demonstrate what God can and will do in spite of our frailty and weakness when we abandon all confidence in our own ability and cast ourselves without reserve upon Him.

The *old covenant* was mechanical, a system of human endeavor, of works and ceremonies. They were only "carnal ordinances, imposed on them until a time of reformation" (Heb 9:10). The *new covenant* was vital, springing from a living inner source. The difference may be illustrated from the growth of a tree and the construction of a house. The house is built section by section from without. The tree is built layer upon layer from within. The stately tree is the spontaneous expression of the hidden life within.

The *old covenant* was studied. Its precepts and prohibitions were coldly and exactly stated. The key words were "Thou shalt" and "Thou shalt not." Obedience was required as a matter of duty. The *new covenant* was spontaneous. To the person living under its gracious provisions, obedience was not a matter of mere duty but of sheer delight. He obeyed the law of God because he now had a disposition that loved to do it. The key word changes from "Thou shalt" to the divine "I will."

The *old covenant* was written on tables of stone. It was a strict law imposed upon man from without and carried a penalty for failure. The *new covenant* is written on the fleshy tables of the heart. Under its terms, the desire and ability to do God's will are incorporated into the believing man's inmost being. It becomes his second nature, the very spring of his choice and desires. "His delight is in the law of the Lord." With his Master he is now able to say, "I delight to do Thy will, O my God."

To sum up, all that the old covenant demands, the new provides. Every defect in the old, occasioned through the weakness of human nature, finds its remedy in the new.

It may cause difficulty for some that this new covenant was to be made with the house of Israel and the house of Judah (Jer 31:31). It could be argued that since this is the case, Gentile believers in this age have no right to claim any benefit under its provisions. The objection is reasonable but finds its adequate answer in Galatians 3:28-29 (ASV): "There can be neither Jew nor Greek, there can be neither bond nor free . . . for ye all are one in Christ Jesus. And if ye are Christ's, *then are ye Abraham's seed*, heirs according to promise."

Through our vital union with Christ, we become inheritors of the spiritual fulfillment of every promise made to Abraham's seed. Abraham was promised in addition to his earthly seed who were to be "as the sand which is upon the seashore," a spiritual seed "as the stars of the heavens" (Gen 22:17). We as his spiritual seed become heirs to all the promised blessings of the new covenant.

## CHARACTERISTICS OF THE NEW COVENANT

### FORGIVENESS

The first and fundamental characteristic of the new covenant is forgiveness: "For I will be merciful to their iniquities, and their sins will I remember no more" (Heb 8:12, ASV; cf. Jer 31:34).

The introductory "for" in this passage indicates that it is the basis of all that precedes. Cleansing of conscience and forgiveness of sin form the indispensable basis of fellowship. We will never reach a state of grace where we will not need the divine mercy. Note the striking contrast between the two covenants in this connection: "But in those sacrifices there is a remembrance again made of sins *every year*" (Heb 10:3); "Their sins . . . will I remember *no more*" (Heb 8:12).

Consider the *freeness* of His forgiveness: "I will be merciful." Think of its *comprehensiveness*: "their iniquities and sins." Rejoice in its *irrevocability*: "no more."

### SANCTIFICATION

The second characteristic is sanctification: "A new heart also will I give you . . . and I will take away the stony heart out of your flesh, and I will give you an heart of flesh. And I will put my spirit within you, and cause you to walk in my statutes" (Eze 36:26-27); "I will put my laws into their mind, and write them in their hearts" (Heb 8:10).

If forgiveness is the fundamental assurance of the new covenant, then sanctification is its central promise.

No longer is the law written on tables of stone, but it is written on the fleshy tables of the believing heart. The teaching here needs no elaboration. God undertakes to impart to us in our inmost being the willingness and desire to do His will. "I will give them an heart to know me" is the promise (Jer 24:7).

This is a sovereign and supernatural operation of the Spirit of God. While we are quite willing to receive at their face value the miracles God has worked in past years, we are often strangely reluctant to do Him the honor of expecting Him to work such a miracle in our own lives. The inevitable result is that we limit Him and He is not able to work a transforming change in us because of our unbelief.

In his book, *The Two Covenants*, Dr. Andrew Murray beautifully illustrated the writing of God's law in the heart:

> The thought of the law written in the heart sometimes causes difficulty and discouragement, because believers do not see or feel in themselves anything corresponding to it. An illustration may help to remove the difficulty.
>
> There are fluids by which you can write so that nothing is visible, either at once or later, unless the writing is exposed to the sun or the action of some chemical. The writing is there, but one who is ignorant of the process cannot think it is there and knows not how to make it readable. The faith of a man who is in the secret knows it is there, though he sees it not.
>
> It is even thus with the new heart. God has put His law into it. "Blessed are the people in whose heart is God's law." But it is there invisibly. He that takes God's promise in faith, knows that it is in his own heart. As long as there is not clear faith on this point, all attempts to find it, or to fulfill that law will be in

vain. But when by simple faith the promise is held fast, the first step is taken to realize it.

If we think that because we have no evidence to our feelings that God has written His law in our hearts, then according to our unbelief will it be unto us. On the contrary, the moment we believe God's promise and act upon it, we will find it true in experience.

God has written His law in the heart of the oak and invariably it produces fruit after its kind—acorns. The fir tree always obeys the law written in its heart and bears fir cones. The migratory bird always obeys the law written in its heart, even though it involves circling the globe. And shall we have the temerity to allege that the same God cannot write His law in the believing heart so effectively that it renders willing obedience?

So then, the God of the new covenant not only forgives the past but assures adequate power to live a life worthy of our high calling in the present. In this way the demands of the old covenant are met in the provisions of the new.

## UNION

The third characteristic is union: "I will be to them a God, and they shall be to me a people" (Heb 8:10).

God's love for His children is such that He does not send a blessing; He brings it Himself. He brings them into vital union with Himself and says that in Him they will find everything that they could expect in a God. In the words of the prodigal's father, He says, "Son, thou art ever with me, and all that is mine is thine." He becomes to us God all-sufficient.

## ILLUMINATION

Last, the new covenant promises illumination: "And

they shall not teach every man his fellow-citizen, and every man his brother, saying, Know the Lord: for all shall know me, from the least to the greatest of them" (Heb 8:11, ASV; cf. Jer 31:34).

Was not this the distinguishing mark of Pentecost? Not so much outward teaching as inward illumination. In the hands of the now Spirit-endued apostles, old scriptures glowed with new light. All seemed to point to and speak of Christ. The promise is that God can be to each believer, the humblest as well as the most highly endowed, the One whom he knows best. *"All shall know me, from the least to the greatest."* What a treasured privilege this covenant bestows—personal access to the great Teacher, personal instruction by the Holy Spirit.

All Christians readily believe and rejoice in the first characteristic of the new covenant, forgiveness, but not all press on to claim their share in the other three. If we have trusted God to fulfill the terms of His covenant as to the forgiveness of our sins, why should we be reluctant to believe that He will keep His promise to write His law in our hearts? It was this very sin of unwillingness to trust the faithfulness of God to His plighted word which excluded Israel from the land of promise: "They could not enter in because of unbelief. *Let us therefore fear,* lest, a promise being left us of entering into his rest, any of you should seem to come short of it" (Heb 3:19; 4:1).

## THE SURETY OF THE COVENANT

A surety is a man who stands good for a weaker friend. He guarantees that an undertaking will be faithfully performed or a financial obligation punctually met. Our Lord stands to us in the relation of surety: "By so much also hath Jesus becomes the surety of a better covenant" (Heb 7:22, ASV).

It need not be said that God will observe His covenant obligations, that He needs no guarantee or surety, but we do. In ourselves we are powerless and weak. Knowing this, our Lord and High Priest offers to make Himself responsible for securing our obedience to the will of God. But He will do this on one condition—that we cease making fresh resolutions, give up unilateral striving and self-effort and cast ourselves on Him without reserve. In response to our trust He will work the miracle, but until we do this He is powerless to help.

L. L. Legters helpfully illustrated the role of the surety. A man is in urgent need of £1,000. He asks the bank manager for a loan of that amount. When questioned about the security he can offer, he has none to give and with scant courtesy he is bowed out of the office. In despair he lays his case before a wealthy friend who drives him into the city to the very same bank. They are greeted by the same officer, but his manner has undergone a remarkable change since the previous visit. Now he cannot do too much. The friend instructs him to advance the £1,000 on his behalf, which he does without demur. The borrower signs a promissory note which is endorsed by his friend. It is the signature of the friend, the surety, and not that of the borrower, which makes the note worth £1,000.

Unfortunately the man is a spendthrift. Before long the money is all gone and he is again in distress. To add to his misery he learns that his wife is dangerously ill in a distant town. He has no money to pay his fare so that he can be with her in her need. The promissory note is due and he receives a demand for payment. In desperation he seeks work and hurries to the bank with £1 he has earned. The official pushes away his £1 and demands £1,000 plus interest. The man's plea that he is doing his best to meet the indebtedness leaves the official unmoved. His wife is dying. At last, in abject despair, he goes once again to his friend and tells all. Again they go to the same bank, the friend hands over his personal check for the amount due and returns to the debtor the discharged note. As surety he has discharged the outstanding obligation. And more than that, he hands the distressed man a check sufficient to enable him to fly to see his wife.

But why did the friend not do this before? Why allow his friend to pass through such an agonizing experience? Because he was trying to pay his own debt and did not confess his need. His surety could do nothing for him until he went confessing his need and seeking his help. Then and only then could he intervene on his behalf.

It may be, because we have been striving to do what He alone can do, that Christ has been unable to fulfill His office as surety of the covenant. Many who are intellectually clear as to the difference between law and grace are not so clear in experience. The great secret of Christian living is to get entirely from under law and to come wholly under the reign of grace.

Under the old covenant the two parties each had their part to play. If either failed, the covenant was broken. Man transgressed the law and broke the covenant. Under the new covenant, however, there is *only one responsible party*—God undertakes all. Note the reiterated divine "I will's." If man had any responsibility under the new covenant other than to receive by faith God's provision, it would no longer be of free grace. It would not be a "better covenant." It is of striking significance that "obey" in the old covenant becomes "believe" in the new. Obedience is still necessary, but it is the obedience of faith. Our part is to believe the astonishing fact that God has written His law in our hearts and will enable us to obey it.

## CONDITIONS OF THE COVENANT

The transition from old to new as a historical fact was not slow or gradual, but was ushered in by the most tremendous crisis in history. The shedding of the blood of Christ terminated the old, while the descent of the Holy Spirit on the day of Pentecost ushered in the new. Preparation for the crisis was slow and long, but the crisis itself, as evidenced in the rending of the veil in the sanctuary, was the work of a moment. Christ's death revealed the utter inefficacy and insufficiency of the old, while Pentecost brought near and imparted all that the new made available.

How can the alluring blessings and liberty of the new covenant become a matter of personal experience? We will neither seek not appropriate them until we are willing to *confess* that we are not enjoying them, that we are still having an old covenant experience. Our own condemning conscience, the knowledge that members of our families or fellow workers have of us, are by themselves sufficient to bring us low before God. We know by experience our own inability to measure up to even what we know of God's demands. Then we will need to *acknowledge* that in the new covenant God has made full provision for every need of our spiritual lives—a heart cleansed from sin, disposed to do the will of God and indwelt by the Spirit. Every weight or sin concerning which God has a controversy with us must be *renounced*, for "if I regard iniquity in my heart, the

Lord will not hear me" (Ps 66:18). It then only remains for faith to *claim* the fulfillment *in us* of the terms of the new covenant. Our eyes will be fixed not so much on the promises of the covenant as on Him who is its surety. As we count on His good faith, we shall experience the blessings of the new covenant which He has sealed with His own blood.

To many it is hard to see what difference it makes whether or not I reckon a thing true. If it be true, it is not such reckoning that makes it true, and if it be false, no reckoning can make it other than false. To many so-called believers, to reckon or count is simply to *imagine*, and implies only credulity, amusing oneself with one's own fancies.

Such entirely miss the true thought that lies behind the word reckon. So far is it from being a mere vain imagination to reckon on God's word as an accomplished fact, that it is the soul and substance of faith.

Seven blessed results may be traced to such reckoning of faith:

1. First of all it is a tribute of faith to God's ability, willingness, love and faithfulness.

2. It is a challenge of faith, indirectly moving God to show Himself the faithful Promiser.

3. It is an attitude of faith, waiting in expectation of blessing.

4. It is, therefore, a removal of limits which unbelief places upon God.

5. It is an opening of the heart to the full reception of promised good.

6. It is the basis of all active obedience and hearty self-surrender.

7. It is the secret of a peaceful, hopeful, courageous triumph over foes.

A. T. PIERSON

# 9

# THE LESSON OF VICTORY

What shall we say then? Shall we continue in sin,
that grace may abound? Sin shall not have dominion
over you: for ye are not under law but under grace
(Rom 6:1, 14).

"AH, THEN, my opponents will cry, we may safely sin,
since we are not under the uncompromising rule of law
but under the lenient sceptre of grace? Out upon the
suggestion!" Thus A. S. Way translates Romans 6:15,
Paul's answer to those who argued that justification by
faith would only serve to encourage a continuance in
sinning. The whole chapter refutes such a contention,
on the grounds that a willful persistence in sinning is
impossible to the justified man because of his union with
Christ in death and resurrection life. The apostle con-
tends that, far from being the ally of sin, grace is its un-
relenting foe and destroyer.

Four answers have been suggested to the initial question of the chapter, "Shall we continue in sin, that grace
may abound?"

> You *cannot*, because you are united to Christ (vv.
> 1-2).
>> Paul is *reasoning*.
> You *need not*, because sin's dominion has been broken
> by grace (vv. 12-14).
>> Paul is *appealing*.

You *must not*, because it would bring sin in again as
Master (vv. 15-19).

Paul is *commanding*.

You *had better not*, for it would end in disaster (vv.
20-23).

Paul is *warning*.

Every Christian is conscious of the power of indwelling sin—"sin that dwelleth in me." He is acutely aware
of the truceless warfare which the old man wages on the
new. While occasionally his efforts have been successful,
more often they have resulted in dismal failure. Many
methods of gaining victory over sin have been adopted,
but without success.

Some have tried to *conquer and subdue* the old life
of nature, and to that end have struggled and wrestled,
fasted and prayed. Sometimes they have been successful. More often they have failed. Human resources
have proved hopelessly inadequate.

Others have endeavored to *tame and starve* it by
rigorous self-discipline and self-denial. Such disciplines
have not been without their beneficial effects, but they
have not produced real and lasting victory.

Others have thought that victory lay in *surrender and
submission* to Christ, and in this they are absolutely
correct, for victory will never be gained without it. As
best they knew how, they have thus surrendered, only
to discover the unsuspected truth that even a surrendered Christian can be a defeated Christian. Surrender
is only negative and we are sanctified not by what we
surrender, but by what we receive.

Still others have expected that in the hour of full
consecration the old nature would be *eradicated* root
and branch, and all disposition to evil for ever removed.
But they have discovered that, while the measure of

their consecration determined the measure of blessing they enjoyed, it did not by any means lift them above the possibility of sinning, and that grievously.

By themselves, none of these methods will give the desired result, although they are immeasurably better than complacency in defeat. Our chapter supplies the key to the problem. The old life must be absolutely *terminated* by death, the death of Christ. "Know ye not that so many of us as were baptized into Christ were baptized into his death? . . . Knowing this that our *old man* was crucified with him" (Ro 6:3, 6, ASV).

Many Christians have yet to learn that there are two sides to the cross of Christ, and they are therefore in the enjoyment of only a half salvation. What a memorable day it was when we saw Christ hanging on the cross, redeeming us, not with shining silver or yellow gold, but with crimson drops of His own precious blood. This is one aspect of the transaction of the cross—*substitution*—summarized in the words, "He loved me and gave himself *for* me." No matter how far we progress in the Christian life, we shall never outgrow this glorious basic fact of our faith.

> All my sins were laid upon Him,
>     Jesus bore them on the tree,
> God, who knew them, laid them on Him,
>     And believing, we are free.

To many, this exhausts the meaning of the cross, but there is a complementary truth of great importance. Christ's death for us on the cross secures deliverance from the guilt and penalty of sin. But the Bible teaches that He not only died for me, but He died *as* me. "I have been crucified *with* Christ, nevertheless I live, yet not I, but Christ liveth in me" (Gal 2:20). In this verse the verb rendered "I am crucified" in the Authorized Version is really in the aorist tense and refers to something that was completed in the past. This is the truth of *identification* with Christ in His death and resurrection, and it is taught just as clearly as the truth of substitution. In Paul's experience, this truth, believed and appropriated by faith, brought complete emancipation from sin's power.

## THE METHOD OF EMANCIPATION—KNOW (vv. 3-11)

In order to experience this deliverance from sin, certain facts revealed in Scripture must be apprehended. The emphasis often falls on *reckoning* ourselves dead to sin, but this reckoning must necessarily be preceded by *knowing* the facts which form the basis of the reckoning. Otherwise it would be imagining rather than reckoning—imagining something to be true which is untrue, instead of counting something to be true which is true. We reckon ourselves to be dead to sin, not in order to become dead to sin, but because, united to Christ, we have died to sin. We can reckon on that fact just as we reckon two and two to be four because they are four. If we know it to be a divinely revealed fact that our former self was crucified with Christ (Ro 6:6, ASV), then reckoning is no effort. If, however, we are not persuaded of this, reckoning it to be so becomes an impossibility.

What facts are we to know? They are three: The meaning of our baptism (v. 3); that our "old man," our former unregenerate self, was crucified with Christ (v. 6, ASV); that we were united with Christ in His resurrection to enjoy an entirely different type of life (v. 4).

It is helpful to compare the method of our deliverance

from sin's guilt and penalty, with that of our deliverance
from its power.

*How were we delivered from the penalty of sin?* By
believing that Christ died *for* us. How do we know that
He died for us? Certainly not because we feel it, for we
were not there to see Him die for us. But as we accept
the testimony of the infallible Word of God on the subject and count on it being true in our case, we enjoy
the assurance of forgiveness.

*How may we be delivered from the power and tyr-
anny of sin?* By believing that we died *with* Christ. How
do we know that we died with Christ? Certainly not
because we feel it. Our feelings might testify to the
contrary. But as we repose our faith in the testimony of
the infallible Word of God to that fact and act accordingly, we will experience the joy of victory over sin.
Our faith rests not in changeful emotional states but on
the immutable Word of God. Crucifixion with Christ is
not an *attainment* of some few advanced believers, but
a *fact* equally true of all Christians though not equally
realized by all. God declares that altogether regardless
of our consciousness of the fact, we were united or
identified with Christ in His death on the cross.

In what sense is it true that we died with Christ? The
answer is found in an understanding of what it means to
be "in Christ." This phrase implies that because we are
united with Him through faith, all that He is in Himself,
and all that He achieved by His death and resurrection,
become ours. Everything that happened to Him is taken
by God as having happened to those who are "in Him."

The teaching of the New Testament is that the believer is united to Christ in a union which though unseen is nonetheless real and vital. Among the figures
used to illustrate this union is that of the vine and its

branches. Vine and branch share exactly the same life. They are organically one. Another figure is that of the head and the body. Christ is the Head and believers are members of His mystical body, each sharing the very same supernatural life. There is also the intimate figure of bridegroom and bride, for we are said to be married to Christ (Ro 7:4). These figures combine to assure us that between us and Christ there exists a vital though mystical union.

The writer of the epistle to the Hebrews provides us with a further illustration of this mystical union.

> Now consider how great this man [Melchisedec] was, unto whom even the patriarch Abraham gave the tenth of the spoils. And as I may so say, Levi also, who receiveth tithes, payed tithes in Abraham. For he was yet in the loins of his father, when Melchisedec met him (Heb 7:4, 9-10).

In expounding Romans 6, Watchman Nee, the noted Chinese Bible teacher, posed this question: "If your great-grandfather had died when he was three years old, where would you be? You would have died in him! Your experience was bound up in his." God has placed us "in Christ" and, in dealing with Christ He has dealt with all who are "in Him." When Christ was crucified, we were crucified because we were in Him. When He died, every member of His body died—hands and feet and head. Thus is it with all who are members of His mystical body.

We must bear in mind, however, that we are identified with Christ not only in His death, but also in His resurrection, with all the resulting blessings (6:5, 8). It is this fact which provides the possibility of walking in newness of life.

THE APPROPRIATION OF EMANCIPATION—RECKON
(vv. 12-14)

If it is true that we died with Christ and rose with
Him, how may we obtain the benefits of this *fait ac-
compli*? The answer of Paul is, *By reckoning*. This is
the word of the mathematician and means simply to
count on a fact as being true. It has nothing whatever
to do with our feelings. If we have doubts about the
fact, we will have consequent difficulty in the reckoning.

The Chinese teacher mentioned earlier graphically
illustrated this point:

> If I were to try and pose as Miss D. I should have
> to say to myself all the time, "You are Miss D. Now
> be sure to remember that you are Miss D." Despite
> much reckoning, the likelihood would be that when I
> was off guard and someone called, "Mr. N.," I should
> answer to my own name. All my reckoning would
> break down at the crucial moment. I *am* Mr. N.
> therefore I have no difficulty whatever in reckoning
> myself to be Mr. N. I can go to sleep and forget all
> about it, but that does not alter the fact. It is as sure
> when I think about it as when I forget it; it is not
> dependent on my memory or my reckoning. When
> anyone calls, "Mr. N.," I spontaneously respond to
> the name, and when any other name is called, with-
> out effort I refrain from answering, for the simple
> reason that I am fully persuaded that I *am* Mr. N. I
> know I am, therefore I naturally reckon it so. Romans
> 6:6 precedes Romans 6:2, not only in the Scriptures
> but in experience too.

WHAT ARE WE TO RECKON?

*That we are dead to sin*: "But I do not feel dead to
sin," our consciousness protests. "How can I reckon
that I am?" The Bible affirms that we are as much

dead to sin now as we ever will be. We know it, not because we feel it, but because God who cannot lie proclaims it as a fact. Note that we are not exhorted to reckon that sin is dead in us—we have painful evidence to the contrary—but that we are dead to sin. There is such power in the mediatorial work of Christ that when we count on this fact, it becomes true in experience. It is for us to believe and consent to what God has done with our old unregenerate self, to agree with His sentence of death upon it. There is no longer any need to struggle against the sinful nature, for *it was terminated at the cross.* Its tyrannical power was broken once for all.

Nowhere in Scripture are we exhorted to crucify ourselves, and for two good reasons. First, because our crucifixion with Christ is always referred to in the past tense. Second, because crucifixion is a form of death which cannot be self-inflicted. Someone else must do it for us. So when Christ was crucified, God saw us as crucified with Him, for we were "in Him" when He died. As our faith lays hold of this precious truth, we become unresponsive to the allurements of our besetting sin, as unresponsive as a dead man. The sin falls off, utterly powerless, not because of any achievement on our part, but through the power of His cross.

We must not, however, live in the atmosphere of the cemetery. A dead man cannot serve God, hence the second part of the apostolic injunction.

*That we are alive unto God.* There flows from Calvary a double stream—a stream of death terminating the dominion of sin, and a stream of life, empowering for holy living. The liberated believer now counts himself alive to all that is holy, dead to all that is sinful; crucified to the world, alive to the church; dead to the dance, alive to the prayer meeting. Appropriating the risen life of Christ, we can say with Paul, "I can do all things through Christ which strengtheneth me." No longer need we impotently cry, "I can't" when called upon to undertake some service for God. As each new demand presents itself, we will in quiet confidence reckon ourselves "alive unto God," and the channels of heart, mind and will will be suffused with divine life. His divine power will become ours through our union with Him. Untold vistas of blessing will open out before us as the Spirit leads us into this "double reckoning."

Sin will reign in our lives only so long as we allow it to reign. We are no longer held in the grip of necessity. "Sin shall not have dominion over you." "Let not sin reign in your mortal body." In itself, sin is utterly impotent. The purpose of our crucifixion with Christ was "that the body as the vehicle of sin might be rendered impotent and become a vehicle of righteousness."

> Buried with Christ and raised with Him too,
> What is there left for me to do?
> Simply to cease from struggling and strife,
> Simply to walk in newness of life,
>     Glory be to God!

> Risen with Christ my glorious Head,
> Holiness now the pathway I tread,
> Beautiful thought while walking therein,
> He that is dead is freed from sin.
>     Glory be to God!

### THE RESULTS OF EMANCIPATION—YIELD
#### (vv. 15-23)

Freedom from sin's dominion is not an end in itself. It is with a view to a new holiness of life and power in service. Are we content to take advantage of the lenient scepter of grace and continue sinning? By no means. We will on the contrary withdraw our members—hands, feet, eyes and tongue—from the service of sin and yield them to God as servants of righteousness.

An initial act of surrender to Christ is presupposed, and this is to be followed by a habitual yielding to His lordship. This daily yielding is the normal and logical outcome of our death and resurrection with Christ. What can we do but joyously yield to the loving Master who has made us "free from sin." The natural result of our emancipation is that we will bring forth "fruit unto holiness" (v. 22). Instead of the repulsive works of the flesh, there is borne the luscious fruit of the Spirit (Gal 5:19-22). The sanctified believer is the only one who enjoys true moral freedom. He can do what he likes!

"Did you say that a sanctified man can do what he likes?" asked one.

"Yes, I did," was the reply.

"Then come with me to the nightclub."

"Ah," was the rejoinder, "but I don't like."

The liberation of the will from the thraldom of sin brings with it the corresponding desire for the will of God alone.

> Living with Christ who dieth no more,
> Following Christ who goeth before,
> I am from bondage utterly freed,
> Reckoning self dead indeed.
>   Glory be to God!
>
> Living for Christ, my members I yield,
> Servants to God for evermore sealed,
> Not under law, I'm now under grace,
> Sin is dethroned and Christ takes its place.
>   Glory be to God!

Growing in Christ, no more shall be named
Things of which now I'm truly ashamed,
Fruit unto holiness will I bear,
Life evermore the joy I shall share.
  Glory be to God!                    T. RYDER

When Abraham Lincoln affixed his signature to the
historic Emancipation Proclamation, every slave in the
United States of America was immediately and auto-
matically released from slavery. From the moment the
ink was dry on the document, every slave was potentially
free. But that did not mean that every slave immediately enjoyed actual liberty. Some masters deliberately
concealed from their slaves the news of their emancipation. Before they experienced their freedom, the slaves
first had to *hear* the good news. Then they had to
*believe* that joyous news, even though it seemed too
wonderful to be true. Next they had to *reckon* on the
fact being true, not of slaves in general, but of themselves in particular. But they could do all this and still
remain slaves. They had to *assert* their freedom and
*refuse* any longer to remain in bondage to their former
masters. In doing this, they could count on the whole
might of the United States being behind them.

Even so must it be with us. We have learned from
the Holy Scriptures that on Calvary Christ signed in
blood drawn from His own veins an emancipation proclamation which potentially freed all believers from the
dominion of sin. It now remains for us to *believe* that
fact, to *reckon* it as being true in our case, and then to
act on it, *refusing* any longer to be slaves of sin. When
we dare to do this, we will find that all the might of the
risen Son of God is on our side, and we will be free indeed. Sin will be powerless to bring us again under its
sway and dominion.

The rest of the spirit, whether it be in action or in repose, consists in its being at harmony with God. Brought by the power of the Holy Spirit into perfect adjustment with the Creator, its affections merged with God's, its will harmonizing with His, there must of necessity be rest.

It is therefore not a rest of inaction, but of harmony of position. The beautiful orbs which adorn the firmament are always in motion, but at the same time they are never in a state of discordance and unrest, because their movements always harmonize with law. They keep up the universal harmony by the exceeding nicety and adjustment of their weights. It is from God's love of law and order that there is produced that divine tranquillity which makes the earth so like a sanctuary. When we have given ourselves as earnestly to the discovery of the laws that govern the tranquillity which is our birthright in the spiritual kingdom as men do to discover the laws that condition harmony in the natural kingdom, we shall know for a certainty what it is to enjoy deep inward repose even amid outward conflict; what Wordsworth describes as

"Central peace subsisting at the heart
Of endless agitation."

J. GREGORY MANTLE

123

# 10

# THE LESSON OF SERENITY

There remaineth therefore a rest to the people of
God. Let us labour therefore to enter into that rest
(Heb 4:9, 11).

WHY DO YOU WANT to be a Christian?" asked Rev. T.
Bompard of a Muhammadan who was seeking Christ.

"There is one verse in the Gospels which alone would
make me wish to be a Christian" was the reply, "the
words of St. Matthew, 'Come unto me, all ye that
labour and are heavy laden, and I will give you *rest*.
Take my yoke upon you, and learn of me; and ye shall
find *rest* unto your souls.' I know the books of Islam,
but there is no promise of rest there. I want that rest."

In the midst of a world of turmoil and violence, of
frustration and disillusionment, there is an inarticulate
and undefined yearning for repose and tranquillity. All
around are anxious hearts and restless feet. As never
before in history, mankind is haunted with fear and
harassed with care. Yet every true disciple of Christ
has been given a sure promise of rest, a rest which is not
always appropriated and enjoyed.

## THE PROMISE OF REST

"Let us therefore fear, lest, a promise being left *us*
of entering into his rest, any of you should seem to come

short of it. We which have believed do enter into rest (Heb 4:1, 3). Rest—in a distressed and distracted world. Rest—in every sorrow and trial and perplexity. Rest—from every care and anxiety. Nothing less than this is promised. Let us not judge what God can do by our past experience but embrace His reassuring affirmation, "There remaineth therefore a rest to the people of God" (Heb 4:9).

The aim of the writer of the epistle to the Hebrews is to illustrate what has been termed "the rest of faith" and to warn his readers of the possibility of falling short of it. He pictures it as a better rest than that into which Joshua led Israel, so it must mean the complete subjugation and dispossession of every foe of the spiritual life. The Spirit-filled Zacharias vividly portrays the characteristics of such a life:

> That we should be saved from our enemies, and from the hand of all that hate us . . . that we being delivered out of the hand of our enemies might serve him without fear, in holiness and righteousness before him, all the days of our life (Lk 1:71, 74-75).

Christ's advent and atonement made possible definite deliverance from all spiritual enemies and the enjoyment of a life of restful service. Nothing less than this is the rest that remains to the people of God, and nothing short of it is true Christian experience. Is this rest the present experience of the reader, or is life a restless striving after an elusive serenity?

### THE PATTERN OF REST

Three "rests" are described in this chapter.

#### CREATION REST

"And God did rest the seventh day from all his

works" (Heb 4:4). The rest enjoyed by God on the seventh day after His transformation of chaos into cosmos was the rest of a completed work, and in it we may discern a foregleam of His method in grace with the new creation. Upon an earth waste and void, the heavenly dove brooded, and from the ruin of a former creation there emerged our wonderful world. "Thus the heavens and the earth were finished, and . . . God . . . rested" runs the record.

It was not that His creative activity had exhausted God and He needed repose, for "the Creator of the ends of the earth, fainteth not, neither is weary." His was the rest of complacency, not of inactivity. Had His purpose in creation not been achieved? Had His ideal not been realized? When an instrument perfectly answers to the designer's mind in its operation, there is rest; the created thing has fulfilled the purpose of its creation. God saw that His work was very good, and He rested, a rest which He invited man to share. But His sabbath rest was soon broken by those with whom He shared it. Adam and Eve, through their tragic choice, forfeited the rest of God for the unrest of "sabbathless Satan," as Milton so aptly styled him.

CANAAN REST

"For if Joshua had given them rest, he would not have spoken afterward of another day" (Heb 4:8), ASV).

*In Egypt.* Israel had found rest from fear of the destroying angel under the sprinkled blood of the Passover lamb. But they were not yet delivered from the tyrannical power of Pharaoh.

*In the wilderness.* They knew rest from the threat of Pharaoh's might, but their experience was the very antithesis of a life of rest. They were endlessly on the move, vacillating between the borders of Egypt and Canaan, perpetually discontented and complaining, but never at rest.

*In Canaan.* They enjoyed a degree of rest never before experienced. Yet in certain important respects it fell short of the divine ideal. Their rest was only partial. It should be remembered that all Israel did not enter Canaan. The whole generation which elected not to cross the Jordan, perished in the wilderness. They were excluded from the enjoyment of God's rest through unbelief, and are a warning to all succeeding generations of the fatal effects of that key sin. "To whom sware he that they should not enter into his rest, but to them that believed not? So we see that they could not enter in because of unbelief" (Heb 3:18-19).

Those whose faith in God was sufficiently strong to induce them to step across Jordan into the land of promise, enjoyed a much better experience—but not God's best. In spite of the divine assurance of victory, and the warning that any inhabitants of the land permitted to remain would be as "pricks in their eyes and thorns in their sides," the Israelites failed to evict and dispossess them. The consequence was that they, too, failed of God's rest.

The evidence of the imperfection of the rest into which Joshua led them was seen in the conditions which prevailed under the rule of the judges—a monotonous cycle of disobedience, disciplines and gracious deliverance.

CHRIST'S REST

"For he that is entered into his rest, he also hath ceased from his own works, as God did from his" (Heb

4:10). Two interpretations of this verse are possible.
One is that the believer ceases to depend on his own
works of law as the means of his sanctification, and
this of course is true. But it seems more probable that
the reference here is not to the believer but to Christ
who is set in contrast to Joshua in verse 8. What
Joshua failed to do, Christ did. As God rested from His
completed work of creation, so Christ ceased from His
finished work of redemption, and now rests! His work
on our behalf having been accepted by God, He has
entered into His rest and sits down at the right hand
of the Father.

Even in His earthly life Christ completely ceased from
His own works, and in this we find a clue to the serenity
of His life:

> I can of mine own self do nothing (Jn 5:30).
>
> My doctrine is not mine, but his that sent me (Jn
> 7:16).
>
> As my Father hath taught me, I speak these things
> (Jn 8:28).
>
> The Father that dwelleth in me, he doeth the works
> (Jn 14:10).

He ceased from His own works and chose to live a
life of complete dependence on His Father. Nor did He
abandon this attitude of dependence until He had accomplished the last detail of His Father's plan and
prayed, "I have glorified thee on the earth: I have finished the work which thou gavest me to do" (Jn 17:4).

For us, this brings the assurance that because He has
entered into His rest, there remains a rest which we too
can enjoy. This is implied in the "for" with which verse
10 begins. We have all rejoiced in Christ's finished work
as the ground of our redemption, but are we rejoicing
in it as the basis of our heart-rest and serenity?

### THE PERIL OF FAILING OF REST

"Let us therefore fear, lest, a promise being left *us* of entering into his rest, any of you should seem to come short of it (Heb 4:1). "Can God . . . ? (Ps 78:19). No Bible book contains more solemn and searching warnings than does this epistle. Let us not lightly gloss over its stern exhortations and admonitions or ingeniously apply them to others. For several reasons Israel came short of God's rest.

#### THEY DOUBTED THE POWER OF GOD

"We be not able to go up against the people; for they are stronger than we" (Num 13:31). Where enemies and potential dangers are concerned, unbelief is a great magnifier. In their consciousness of the superior power and prowess of their foes, the Israelites completely lost sight of the almightiness of their God which had so frequently been exercised on their behalf.

#### THEY DISTRUSTED THE LOVE OF GOD

"Would God that we had died in the land of Egypt! Or . . . in this wilderness! . . . our children should be a prey" (Num 14:2-3). Unbelief has a singularly short memory for the promises and providences of God. In spite of repeated and unforgettable evidences of His loving care and protection, they treated Him as though He were utterly unreliable instead of unchangingly trustworthy.

#### THEY DISBELIEVED THE WORD OF GOD

"For indeed we have had good news preached to us, just as they also; but the word they heard did not profit them, because it was not united by faith in those who heard" (Heb 4:2, NASB). Unbelief has a weak digestion where the Word of God is concerned. Where it is present in the heart, the Word, instead of nourishing the spiritual life, produces a hardness and insensitiveness to the voice of God. Before we condemn the Israelites too much, let *us* therefore fear lest there be in *us* an evil heart of unbelief in departing from the living God (3:12).

## The Pursuit of Rest

This sounds strangely paradoxical, and yet it is a correct conception. Rest does not just happen. It requires diligent and persevering pursuit. "Let us labour therefore to enter into that rest, lest any man fall after the same example of unbelief" (Heb 4:11).

It is not so much labor in the sense of working which is in view here, as that of ceasing from our own working and allowing God to work in us. This will require great diligence on our part. In describing his own experience, Paul says, "I labour, striving according to *his* energy, who energizes in me in might" (Col 1:29, par).

> I struggled and wrestled to win it,
> The blessing that setteth me free,
> But when I had ceased from my struggles,
> His peace Jesus gave unto me.

There came a time in the experience of J. Hudson Taylor, founder of the China Inland Mission (now Overseas Missionary Fellowship), when the burdens, both personal and incidental to his position as director of a pioneer missionary society, threatened to overwhelm him. Added to these was an intolerable sense of inward failure. He described his state at this time in the following words:

> I prayed, agonized, strove, made resolutions, read

the Word more diligently—but all was without effect. Every day, almost every hour, the sense of sin oppressed me. . . . Then came the question, "Is there no rescue? Must it be thus to the end—constant conflict and instead of victory, too often defeat?"

He then described the way in which the Lord gently led him into rest and victory. He saw that it all hinged upon simple faith in Christ to lead him into the promised rest. But he did not have this faith.

But how to get faith strengthened? *Not by striving after faith, but by resting on the Faithful One.* As I read, I saw it all! "If we believe not, He abideth faithful." I looked to Jesus and saw (and when I saw, oh, how joy flowed!) that He had said, "I will never leave you." Ah, *there* is rest, I thought. I have striven in vain to rest in Him. I'll strive no more.

And how did this new experience work out in the daily detail of his life? He tells the sequel.

The sweetest part is the *rest* which full identification with Christ brings. I am no longer anxious about anything. . . . So if God place me in great perplexity, must He not give me much guidance; in positions of great difficulty, much grace; in circumstances of great pressure and trial, much strength?

It was at this time that his favorite hymn was

Jesus, I am resting, resting,
In the joy of what Thou art,
I am finding out the greatness
Of Thy loving heart.

### THE PATHWAY TO REST

"We which have believed *do enter* into rest. Seeing therefore it remaineth that some *must* enter therein.

. . . To day, if ye will hear his voice, harden not your hearts" (Heb 4:3, 6-7).

If this rest is available, and some do enter in and some must enter in, why not you? God does not tantalize His children and hold out a prospect which is impossible of fulfillment. Charles Wesley realized that this rest was entered by an act of faith when he sang:

> Lord, I believe a rest remains
> To all Thy people known;
> A rest where pure enjoyment reigns
> And Thou art loved alone.
>
> O that I now that rest might know,
> *Believe*, and enter in:
> Now, Saviour, now the power bestow,
> And let me cease from sin.

Dr. Andrew Murray suggested these simple steps to enter into this rest.

*I believe there is a life of rest* into which Jesus, my heavenly Joshua, can lead me. It is doubt that effectively closes the door on a life of rest.

*I am not enjoying that rest.* Be honest with God. No progress will be made until there is honest confession of failure. Acknowledge that, like Israel, you have been unbelieving and disobedient, and therefore have failed of His rest.

*That life of rest is for me.* Do you protest that your character is too unstable, your will too weak, your temperament too hasty, and that such a life is not for you? Do you limit God through your unbelief, and measure His power by your past experience? God has no favorites. What any other believer has received from God, you may have. This life is possible for you.